MW00954112

A Beautiful Moon Waiting

An Adoption Memoir

Ashley Banion

A Beautiful Moon Waiting
An Adoption Memoir

Copyright © 2020 by Ashley Banion

All rights reserved. No part of this book may be reproduced or transmitted in any form or by any means, electronic or mechanical, including photocopying and recording, or by any information storage and retrieval system, without permission in writing from the author.

First Edition, November 2020

ISBN- 9798697389492

1. Nonfiction - Memoir 2. Nonfiction - Adoption & Fostering 3. Nonfiction - Family & Relationships

Published by Ashley Banion
Printed and distributed through Kindle Direct Publishing

Cover design by Vince Banion
Editing by Jonathan Jordan | Wordrobe Media
    www.wordrobemedia.com

Dedication Page

To Everly…you truly are the moon to our night sky. May you always know that even though you had no control over your past, your future can be anything you want it to be. We love you more than life.

CONTENTS

PROLOGUE | This Is Us   2

CH. 1 | Research, Research, Research   9

CH. 2 | Stormy Times   21

CH. 3 | Learning to Grieve, Learning to Cope   35

CH. 4 | Emotional Whiplash   49

CH. 5 | The Perfect Storm   59

CH. 6 | An Ocean of Grief   70

CH. 7 | Maybe You're Wrong   80

CH. 8 | Just Keep Going   90

CH. 9 | Having Faith   94

CH. 10 | She's Here, and She's Perfect   104

CH. 11 | Not Leaving   112

CH. 12 | Blessings and Blowouts   122

CH. 13 | The Journey Ends   128

CH. 14 | Moving Forward   142

EPILOGUE | Here and Now   147

ACKNOWLEDGEMENTS | 152

ABOUT THE AUTHOR   154

Prologue: This Is Us

Dear Future Little One,[1]

Most days, I feel as if I will never find my way to you. I imagine the day our eyes will meet for the very first time and the way my heart will be forever yours and never again belong to me.

I envision what you will look like and what type of little personality you will have. Some days I feel as if the day your daddy and I have been waiting for will never come and I lose hope...

I'm sorry for that.

I'm sorry that my fear overcomes my excitement and my doubts cloud my faith. Your momma tries so hard to stay strong, but some days, the fight feels impossible. But then I am reminded of whom I'm fighting for and I am rejuvenated. I feel as if I could fight forever. I know without a doubt that in the end, this journey will all be worth it...you will be worth it.

I promise to try to do better, to be stronger, and to not lose sight of what is waiting for us at the end of this long, difficult road. Your daddy and I don't know when you will come. We do know each day brings us one step closer to you. We long for the day we get to wrap our arms around you and never have to let go. We love you so much already, in the most incredible way, and we have faith we will find you soon.

And when that day arrives, I know our souls will recognize one another and we will forever be changed for the better.

Love,

Your momma

---

[1] From our blog, posted July 27, 2017

I think I started and deleted the beginning of this book about a hundred times. So if you are reading this, that means I finally finished it. If I have done what I set out to do, you will smile, cry, laugh, and hopefully be inspired by this crazy — almost unbelievable — story of ours.

Junior Prom

So why not start at the beginning?

Vince and I are high school sweethearts. I know, I know, in this day and age, that is extremely rare, but I kid you not. We grew up and have always lived in a very small, rural village in Ohio. Our village of less than 3,000 people is the kind of place where kids legitimately drive tractors to high school one day a year, and where the average graduating class is sixty students or fewer. I can't make this stuff up, people.

Anyway, I digress...

We went to school together from kindergarten through senior year but didn't start dating until the summer before our junior year. Actually, let me take you back to our very first date...

We were on our way to the local putt-putt and ice-cream hangout in Vince's 1996 forest green Pontiac Grand Am with the windows down and the R&B music blaring through the speakers he had specially put in the car for the bass. We thought we were so cool.

Even though I told him to take the highway, he chose to take the curvy backroads. Around a tight curve, I saw a tiny bunny hopping across the road. I expected him to slam on his brakes like I would do, but nope...he hit the bunny! And I cried.

When I say I cried, I mean I sobbed.

3

I am pretty sure Vince thought I was crazy, and I was so embarrassed. I kept repeating something incomprehensible about how the cute little bunny was just trying to live its life and we killed it. I kind of thought he was a monster.

Now, before you start thinking he is a monster, I should probably clarify that he did not even see the bunny. Apparently, not everyone scans the road for tiny animals while driving like I do. Who knew?

Needless to say, I am an animal lover, and Vince figured that out pretty quickly.

Anyway, Vince had no words, but he really tried to console me. Instead of taking me home, he took me to get ice cream, and while looking in the gift shop, he bought me a small Precious Moments figurine of three little bunnies sitting together. What he did not know at the time was that I was an avid collector of those figurines because my great-grandma always gave them to me for special occasions. It was something that meant so much to me. I actually still have that figure on display with the rest of my Precious Moments collection.

This was my first glimpse into the person Vince is...he is a fixer. He tries so hard to make everything alright and to fix anything that is wrong or broken. This became even more evident years later as our adoption journey unfolded. It is one of his personality traits that I love most.

Vince and I ended up going to the same small private college only twenty minutes from home. We both studied middle childhood education with specialization in English and social studies, so we took most of our classes together.

Once we both graduated from college in 2006, I was lucky enough to land a job right away in my beloved hometown teaching fifth grade English at the very same elementary school I attended. Because I had been a cheerleader since third grade and all the way through college, I also took over for my high school cheer coach and began coaching the sport I love with all my heart.

Vince began teaching part-time at a local school as well and later became full-time. He has also coached just about everything over the years: football, baseball, basketball, and golf.

For the first couple years after graduating, people questioned why we hadn't married yet. You have to understand that where we come from, it is not uncommon to get married shortly after college — or even high school. But with Vince only having a part-time job and because his father had been diagnosed with cancer shortly before we graduated from college, we had decided to put marriage on hold until we saved some money and so he could spend more time with his family. Vince has always been family-oriented, and the idea of losing his father affected him greatly. He took on many of the responsibilities so that his dad could focus solely on fighting the cancer.

Unfortunately, Vince's dad passed away in January of 2009, but I'm still so thankful Vince had the opportunity to live at home all those years and could spend his time devoted to his father and the rest of his family.

Wedding Day

We became officially engaged in February 2009, and on October 16, 2010, we tied the knot in a small country ceremony, complete with me wearing white cowboy boots. Don't let your imagination carry you away, it wasn't a super tacky, over-the-top themed wedding. It turned out to be a beautiful fall day (FYI, fall is my favorite season) and was exactly what we envisioned — crisp leaves and pumpkins galore, caramel-dipped apples, and pumpkin spice everything.

"First comes love, then comes marriage, then comes a baby in a baby carriage."

Yeah, yeah, I know the old rhyme and, believe it or not, at our wedding reception we had people ask when we would start a family. Really?

I understood the reasoning...in our little village, it is not uncommon for couples to get married and pregnant both in the same year. There is nothing wrong with that, but it just wasn't what we had envisioned for our future. I really wanted a few years of just Vince and me, where we could enjoy married life and each other without our entire lives revolving around tiny little humans.

Plus, we were not mature enough for kids...yeah, we were twenty-six years old, but we lived the first eight months of married life with my parents, for goodness' sake. In June of 2011, we bought our first house, renovated it, and moved in right after the school year ended.

Vince will tell you that by the beginning of 2012, he was ready for kids. I was as well, at least to some extent, but I really felt I wanted a different approach to growing our family. Whenever I pictured our family growing, I always saw adoption. I was terrified to mention it to Vince though, which is ludicrous considering we had been together since we were just babies (well, basically) and had talked about how we would love to adopt one day. I shouldn't have been scared to tell him anything, but I suffer from anxiety, and my fears are sometimes irrational. More on that later...

I became hyper-aware of the orphan crisis during high school and even told one of my best friends that I would adopt a baby girl from an Asian orphanage one day, a story she just recently reminded me of.

Without telling Vince, I began researching domestic and international adoption. I cannot tell you why, but I could not get it out of my mind. I felt drawn to adoption even though nobody in my family has ever been adopted. I honestly can't even remember the first defining moment when adoption was placed in my heart. Maybe it has just always been there, just a part of who I am.

After years of research, discussion, and a hundred calls and emails to agencies, we made our decision and stepped onto the path that led us to where we are today.

Our year-long journey was full of ups and downs; it was nowhere near easy or perfect, and it was definitely not a fairytale. In some ways, it was the worst year of our lives and in others, one of the very best. I'm not here to lie to you and tell you how amazing and perfect the last few years have been — I'm here to tell you about a journey we chose, a road we volunteered to go down. And I'm here to tell you that it was hard, it was beautiful, and it is something I would sign up to do a thousand times again.

PART I

The Decision

CHAPTER 1

Research, Research, Research

Choosing International Adoption[2]

"The first question most people ask is, "Why adoption?" and the second is, "Why international adoption?" Our answer is simply that we don't really know. The short response is because we feel drawn to international adoption, but I am not going to pretend that I understand why we have been drawn to this. Maybe it's because all kids are worthy of a home and parents to love them and God has chosen us for this journey. Maybe it's simply because we are being led to where our child is waiting for us."

In May of 2012, I had the amazing opportunity to tag along with my brother and mom when they traveled to Japan. Anyone who knows me at all, knows this was way out of my comfort zone.

Me with my brother, Terry, in Japan in 2012

I am the girl who once actually skipped a college class simply because I could not walk into the classroom after everyone else was there and seated. Planes terrify me, so the thought of a twelve to thirteen hour plane ride about killed me. I mean, seriously, I know they

---

[2] From our first blog post on our website, posted June 3, 2016.

are supposed to be safer than riding in a car, but in my eyes, if a plane is going down, it will definitely be the one I am on. Are you sensing how debilitating my anxiety is yet? I am talking full-blown panic attacks...tunnel vision, hot flashes, damp skin from sweat, wheezing, trembling, elephant-on-my-chest panic attacks.

But I conquered my fears and hopped on the plane to head to a strange place, not knowing anyone or even more than three words of the language. The first day was rough — like, really rough — but after that, it was amazing!

Our pilot did not show up for the first flight, therefore we were rerouted to Chicago and then San Francisco. That put us a day behind, so we lost money on a canceled night at the hotel and the first tour we were supposed to take. Oh, and of course our luggage was left behind in Chicago for two days. Why not make this more stressful for me?

Once we discovered our luggage was lost, we had no other option except to find our way to the hotel. Unfortunately, it took us several hours to get two miles from the train station after leaving the airport. Why, you say? Oh, because we couldn't navigate our way out of the station. We legitimately were stuck and could not get the gates to let us out.

After finally receiving help from a very friendly Japanese man, we walked to our hotel and checked in. My mom then proceeded to lock herself in the bathroom and cry that she wanted to go home for about an hour. She was tired and frustrated that everything was not going as planned. Good times.

But honestly, it truly was an amazing trip after that rocky start to the trip.

While in the beautiful country of Japan, I felt complete peace and at home for reasons I could

Mt. Fuji in 2012

not even really explain. I still can't explain it. I completely fell in love with Japan and its people, and when we left, it was as if I knew I would be back there someday. I didn't know how or when, but I knew I had to come back — and I had to bring Vince.

At the beginning of 2013, I finally opened up and told Vince I wanted to consider adoption. Not only was he completely open to it, but he even mentioned that he wanted to pursue adoption as well. I filled him in on what I had been researching and the pros and cons of domestic and international adoption and the countries we might consider.

We debated on whether to try for a biological child first or to go the adoption route first, and then we also had to consider what country...China, America, South Korea, Ethiopia, and a couple others.

> "For three years, I did research into countries and agencies. I emailed asking questions and talked to people who had adopted. I read hundreds of blogs as well. At the time, four of my friends and acquaintances had or were in the process of adopting domestically and internationally. As I was gaining information and informing Vince of what I was finding out, I still had reservations.
>
> For someone like me, someone who suffers from anxiety, the idea of adoption is terrifying. For those who suffer with anxiety, control is very important; we need to have control in order to keep the anxiety and panic at bay. There is no greater loss of control than during the adoption process. Dealing with the unknown, the delays, the court process, the paperwork, the governments of two countries, etc. Maybe this was the cause of my reservations, for the delay of taking that step. Maybe it was also the fact that this was so unconventional."

After I had been actively researching adoption, I decided to research Japanese adoption, even though I had never heard of it. I stumbled across two agencies in America that had small Japanese programs and contacted both.

One agency informed me that the program was full and would most likely stay closed to new applicants for at least five to six years. The other agency informed me that they were aiming to grow their program and were hoping to open to new applicants in one to three years, at most.

"In some ways, if I'm being completely honest, I was afraid that Vince wasn't truly on the same page as me. I was afraid he was just trying to make me happy by going along with this crazy dream of mine. To this day, whether it is my anxiety or just my personality, I still let that fear creep up and threaten to strangle me. This isn't a new car or a new television. This is our child, a child we will love and cherish for the rest of our lives. This is the biggest decision of our lives.

Another fear is the money. How in the world would two school teachers afford to adopt? The idea of fundraising, asking for donations, saving every penny, applying for grants, and possibly taking out a loan, is almost paralyzing.

But even through the fear of what others might think or say, the fear of the unknown and of the adoption process, the fear of trying to find a way to afford it, my heart still wants what it wants, and right now, it wants to adopt a beautiful child who might otherwise never know the love of a family. My heart feels as if our child is already waiting for us, as impossible as that sounds. It's amazing how your heart can be in love with an idea, with something or someone it hasn't even seen yet. But I promise you all, it can happen.

When we first discussed this seriously, we were drawn to Japan, since we were comfortable with that country, but realized that the list was still not open after several years of being closed. We ruled out most of the African countries because of the government delays and/or long stays in country. Both of us being teachers and coaches with several animals to take care of, we knew we needed to be in country less than two weeks if at all possible.

So through research and talking with agencies, we narrowed the search down to Taiwan and China. We feel as if both countries have called to us, but we felt the pull of China a little more. Gendercide in China is more common than most are aware of, and the high number of orphans in China is staggering."

If I can give any advice, it would be to do your research. We researched agencies online and through talking with others who had gone through the adoption process. Research and ask for recommendations until it feels right to you. I would say until you have no doubts, but in the world of adoption, a part of you will always have some fear over what you cannot control. You might fear it will take longer than expected, that the program might shut down unexpectedly, you may not get the money to proceed, or the million other unknowns.

We completely fell in love with one agency and the assistant director. She never once tired of answering my millions of questions and we knew we wanted to work with them because of the trust we had developed with them.

We decided to contact them and start the process, but again our plans were changed. God intervened once more...

> "The wonderful lady who I have been relentlessly bugging with hundreds of questions for three years, informed me that Japan was getting ready to open to possibly ten more applicants.
>
> Vince and I talked about it for nearly four weeks. We prayed so hard for the answer, for a sign. We kept debating and going back and forth. I finally realized God was sending us signs, small signs almost every day...
>
> Vince and I sat down and really talked about it. We feel like our hesitation may have led us to this moment because maybe Japan was always where we were meant to adopt from."

A few weeks later, Vince and I told the assistant director, Kelsey, we thought the Japan program reopening was the sign we were looking for and asked for the application. That was our first choice, and that is the choice that felt right to us.

It is amazing to me how the universe, God, fate, all intervene and lead you right to the place you were always meant to be.

We were officially accepted in the middle of May 2016 and began our home study at the end of July. It looked as if Vince would be traveling to Japan after all, and it would be for the most incredible reason.

> "So at this time, we feel adopting a son or daughter from Japan is what God intends for us. This does not mean we will never have biological children as well or that we won't adopt domestically in the future; it simply means that we are choosing to start our family in what some may believe to be the untraditional way. So if you are wanting and willing to take this journey with us, feel free to follow our blog as we bring home our baby girl or boy in the near future."

Anxious

Anxiety…it's real. I know because there have been moments, days, weeks of my life where I have felt completely debilitated by it. For a long time, I told myself to just get over it, that it wasn't a real thing, that if people knew how messed up I really was, they would think I was completely crazy.

But then I hit thirty years old and I realized it was getting worse; I could not turn off my feelings or the panic I felt at times. I constantly felt as if something bad was bound to happen at any moment, but I had no idea what it was. Anxiety is completely irrational, but it is so very real. So I read blogs about it, I read books about it, I talked to others about it, and that's when I knew that anxiety was not some made up diagnosis. That's when I knew that I had to take my life back.

The reason I am telling you this is because anxiety held me back for a long time. I truly care what people think, and that is what led to the feelings of trepidation.

It took me months to work up the courage to tell close friends and family about our decision, and then once Vince and I decided to take the leap, it took me an entire month to write my first two blog posts and to actually share them with others. Okay, I guess I should be completely honest here...I wrote up a post and shared our blog on social media at 11:30 at night...I proceeded to turn my phone on silent and went straight to bed. I was too frightened, too anxious to read the comments. Fear and anxiety took over my body to the point where I actually felt sick.

When I woke the next morning, I realized I had several missed texts and close to one hundred notifications on my social media accounts. My heart was racing, my vision was blurry, and I felt as if I would vomit, but I read every message and comment with tears streaming down my cheeks and was blown away by the support we were receiving.

That's when I realized we could do this and that my anxiety could be beaten; I just had to take control and fight like hell to achieve my goals and the life I wanted to live, and most importantly, I had to just live because we only get one life; we might as well live it the way we want.

After announcing we were adopting from Japan, we received several questions, but the most frequent and common questions were "Why Japan?" or "You can adopt from Japan?" or even "Is there really a need for families to adopt from Japan?"

Our response was very detail-oriented and probably more informative than most people were looking for, so we decided to write a blog post about it so anyone who would like to read about it could do so, and those who wanted a short response could hear us simply say, "Yes, there is a need, it is legal, and because we feel drawn to Japan; we believe that is where our child is waiting for us."

Choosing Japan and the Process[3]

"There are an estimated 147 million orphans in the world. Most people see the need of the people living in China and India because of the gendercide against girls. Or in African countries that suffer from war, civil unrest, and famine. But most do not think of Japan as a country where there is a need for international adoption. So some may be wondering why we chose Japan. The simple answer goes back to my last post...we feel drawn there, because that is where our child is. The longer, more detailed answer is that there is a need in Japan, even if it doesn't seem so."

Japan is a stunningly beautiful country. It is rich in culture and history, and the Japanese people are helpful, thoughtful, smart, and kind. Unfortunately, some historical practices of Japan are still very much intact. In a sense, culturally, some may feel that they have not left the times of the early 1900s.

As was explained to us by our agency, blood relations and the purity of women are still thought to be extremely important in the Japanese culture. Many Japanese people just do not understand why anyone would want to adopt a child who is not a blood relative; therefore, a staggering number of children spend their entire childhood in an orphanage or institution. Japan has an extremely low number of foster homes and people willing to adopt domestically. Thousands of kids never know what it is like to have a family. At the age of eighteen, they are allowed to leave the institution, but there is nobody there to guide them through life. Many never go to college, and very few hold a steady job.

Then there is the stigma that surrounds a woman who has a child out of wedlock in Japan. She is thought to have brought shame to her entire family. Because of this, many women and girls have abortions or move away until they have the baby, which is then placed in an orphanage. It's not that they don't love their babies; it's actually the complete opposite — but they have very few other options. These women may never have the

---

[3] From our second blog post on our website, posted June 8, 2016.

support of their families and will never have a future, so the mindset is that the baby will have a better life in the safe environment of an orphanage. In Japan, once a woman has a baby, it becomes difficult for a woman to find a husband because they are now sometimes considered shameful or ruined.

There are organizations present in Japan that are trying to change these decades-old practices and beliefs, but like everything, change takes time. There is one such agency in Japan trying to make positive changes. They provide counseling for expectant mothers who do not want to have an abortion. This agency provides housing for the expectant mothers, healthcare for the mother and the baby, and then helps the mother make a plan for her baby.

The first priority is to help the mother keep her baby. The next option is to help find a relative or another family in Japan willing to adopt the baby. The final option is international adoption. This is to help keep children out of orphanages, so they have the best chance at a happy, successful life.

> "This agency works with our agency here in America. If they have a mother who wants her child adopted here in the US, our agency has a list of waiting families. The birth mother, or first mom, actually has the opportunity to meet the adoptive family and learn more about them. This is such a special and amazing opportunity for both the birth mother and the adoptive parents.
>
> The Japan program is very unique. Once we get a referral (which should be in the next twelve months), we travel within two to three weeks. Our baby will most likely be between four to eight weeks old at the time we bring him or her home. As the adoptive parents, we have the privilege of possibly meeting the birth mother while in Japan and getting to know the background of the birth parents, including medical history and just basic likes and dislikes of the birth mother and her family. We will be in Japan for approximately one week and the adoption is finalized here in our home state approximately six months after returning home.

There are many other details I could share about Japan and the reasons why international adoption is needed, but it's not my story to tell. We are just one piece of the puzzle. I stand by the belief that Japan is an amazing country filled with amazing people. The culture is what makes their country so beautiful and ironically, also what makes international adoption necessary. My hope is that in the coming years, the need for international adoption will diminish and that more children in Japan will stay with their biological families, but until that day comes, many people will fight for those who cannot fight for themselves. There will soon be one less orphan in Japan."

Now that I have told you our backstory, let's return to the end of that May, 2016...by Memorial Day weekend we had filled out and mailed back our application and had been officially accepted into the program. We received our welcome packet with tons of paperwork to complete and information to read. Vince and I diligently filled out every form sent to us and contacted our home study agency here in Ohio as soon as we decided on the right one for us.

For us, we needed to work with two agencies here in the US, along with the Japanese agency in Tokyo. The reason for that is because our adoption agency here in America was located outside of our state, so in order to have a home study completed, we needed this third agency to conduct home visits and interviews to approve us to adopt. The completed and approved home study would then be sent to our placement agency out of state and then sent to the government agency known as Citizenship and Immigration Services (or USCIS), along with other necessary paperwork, so we could officially be approved and placed on the wait list for a referral.

Are you still with me? Yeah, it's a lot.

So, like we did for our placement agency, we researched and emailed home study agencies throughout the spring, but once we were accepted into the program, we spent all of June speaking to home study agencies all across Ohio...we just could not decide which option was best for us.

Just when we were about ready to play a game of "Eeny Meeny Miny Mo," I had an idea. I had an amazing friend from high school who was in the exhausting process of bringing home her two adopted children from the Democratic Republic of the Congo. I texted her asking what home study agency she used and why. She gave me the name of a smaller agency up north that had a second small office only forty minutes from us. I sent an email immediately and received a response the next day.

The standard response was given: "We have never done a home study for a Japan adoption, and we aren't sure what is involved, but we would love to help you." We chose them for multiple reasons, such as cost, integrity, availability, and how quickly they could start our home study. They reached out to to our placement agency and together, we all learned what was needed to complete a home study for Japan, which was actually very similar to most other countries.

In July, we filled out the paperwork needed for our home study agency and took our online classes. These classes informed us of the orphan crisis, the need for assistance and families all across the world, the bonding and anxiety and language barriers these children must hurdle, the challenges children face while in orphanages, the emotional and mental toll the adoption process takes on the adoptive parents, and so many other topics. To be honest, it scared us, but it also helped us, and more than anything, it emboldened our resolve in our decision to give a child in need a home.

Vince and I felt like most of these issues would not pertain to us entirely. For example, in the Japan program, newborns between four to eight weeks of age are placed with permanent, loving families, and the first mom has a say in the adoptive family for the baby. Most of the time, the expectant mothers find the agency in Japan once they have exhausted their options or if they are just unable to raise their baby on their own. Japan's culture is very complex and can feel somewhat outdated by us Americans, while also feeling completely unique and enticing.

Our future little one would not have to live in an orphanage, per se, but would live in a baby room in an office building, with nannies available at all times until our arrival in Tokyo. Even though our little one would most likely not face as many challenges as some orphans across the world, we were glad we were prepared, and we were happy our eyes were opened to the reality of everyday lives for many children all around the world.

It seemed as if the only thing possibly standing in our way now was my own anxiety and fear. How was I ever going to push through?

I knew what I wanted, what we both wanted, but the fear and worry haunted me at night. I knew I had to find a way, but sometimes my doubts and anxiety crept back in and settled inside me threatening to destroy everything we wanted:

> "Am I strong enough to get out of my own way? Can I allow myself to go after the one thing I have wanted for as long as I can remember? How will we work through this?"

CHAPTER 2

Stormy Times

Let's move forward to the beginning of August, 2016. We had finally settled on a home study agency and were scheduling our initial home visit.

We were so incredibly nervous but had a good feeling. Then my whole world stopped...

Enjoying the Wait[4]

"On August 1, we took our precious Sheltie boy, Stormy, to the vet for an annual checkup. He seemed completely healthy, so we thought it would be a routine checkup. Since he is nine, we decided to have blood work done to get him checked out. That was a Monday; on Thursday, our vet called us with some surprising and unsettling news... Storm's kidney and liver enzymes were elevated. They were not off the charts, but enough that it was very concerning to our vet. We had to get him on two antibiotics for bacterial infections and on a special kidney diet. Of course, I instantly began researching kidney and liver disease and other causes of the elevated levels. Most of what I read was disheartening, to say the least, and completely overwhelming."

I felt as if a piece of my heart and soul died after hearing his grim

---

4 Our blog post, August 20, 2016.

diagnosis. Losing him was incomprehensible, and I was afraid the rest of me would die right along with him.

I know that some people won't resonate with this, and that's okay. But I know some of you will get it...some of you will understand the connection I had to "my boy" as I often called him. As cliché as it sounds, he was family to me. He was the one I told my secrets to and the one who always made me feel better when I felt down or weak.

To be completely real with you, I had never felt so lost, so terrified. I didn't know what to do or how I would ever live without him. At that point, nothing seemed to matter, yet in just a couple of days, I was supposed to put on a smiling face and assume the role of the most stable person in the world for a social worker, while inside I felt as if I were drowning or screaming out in a crowded room at the top of my lungs, yet nobody could hear me.

> "Over the next week and a half, I delved into my research; I found diet and nutrition information, as well as holistic treatment approaches to try to combat kidney disease. I also began making homemade dog food and switched to distilled water only for our pets. I made his follow-up appointment for more blood work and another appointment with a holistic veterinarian for acupuncture and Chinese herbal remedies."

I was desperate. When I wasn't researching ways to help Stormy, I was holding on to him for dear life, willing the tears to stop falling. To this day, I still don't think anyone fully comprehends the level of utter hopelessness, fear, and complete devastation I truly felt.

> "Now to be raw and real with you all...I have been a complete mess. My anxiety has me thinking the worst and picturing what I am going to do and how I can keep him healthy and with us for many more years. I cannot concentrate on ANYTHING else. I feel like a walking zombie. All I do is cry and worry.

> Getting through the first week of school was torture for me. I felt

so guilty while at school, simply because I want to do nothing but spend time with him. He could have months or he could have years. The unknown is debilitating.

I find myself hating and cringing at the phrase, 'I can't wait until..." Why? Because I can wait. We spend our whole lives hoping and waiting for something else to happen, and some day, we will turn around and realize our days are numbered and we didn't even enjoy the ride. Enjoying the ride is so very hard for someone like me, someone who worries constantly about the future and what tomorrow will look like. For someone who worries nonstop, but doesn't even know why she's worried. But I am making a conscious effort to stop wishing my life away, to enjoy and relish every single day. That is so much easier said than done though."

Then the day came for our home study, and I was determined to make sure our social worker would see the loving parents we could be, not the disaster I felt like I was becoming.

We had a two-day notice before our home study was to take place. We were beyond stressed and panicking hard. We were trying to enjoy the adoption process, but we had no idea what to expect when the social worker walked through our door. We decided we needed help.

A friend, Beccie, texted me a message about everything her social worker looked for in the house: fire extinguishers, smoke and carbon monoxide detectors, emergency contacts, and fire escape plans to name a few.

I thanked her profusely, then texted one of my dearest friends, Kalyn, to ask her advice on fire extinguishers since her husband was a firefighter. She was willing to drop everything to come over to help us prepare and even offered to buy anything we needed on her way.

After speaking with Beccie and Kalyn, I remember looking at Vince. I'm not sure what he saw in my eyes when his met mine, but he quickly wrapped me in a strong embrace and said the words I desperately needed to hear, "We have two full days and nowhere else to be. We'll get it done and everything will be fine."

I didn't say anything. I just nodded and took a deep breath. I needed to feel in control of something. I needed to feel like I was able to accomplish one task. I just needed to feel worthy.

While Vince ran out to pick up the carbon monoxide detector and the two fire extinguishers Kalyn had suggested, I typed up an emergency contact list to place on our refrigerator along with the fire escape plan. Together we chipped away at the list of items that needed to be completed, and then scrubbed and polished every inch of our house.

We checked our fence in the backyard to make sure it was stable and safe, fixed a small crack in our drywall, double-checked the locks on every door and window, and baby-proofed the cabinets with locks that I myself can barely maneuver to this day, and padded the furniture's sharp edges with foam. We were exhausted by the end of day two and fell asleep as soon as we hit the bed.

The home study visit took place the next morning on August 10 and took a little over two hours. The first few awkward minutes may have been the worst. We opened the door with unnatural smiles plastered on our faces. Taylor, our social worker, smiled back at us from where she stood on the porch. We welcomed her in and ushered her to the kitchen table.

Vince awkwardly asked, "Would you like some cookies?"

He held out a plate of store-bought cookies we picked up at the last minute.

Taylor chuckled and kindly responded, "No, thank you. I appreciate the offer, but you have no idea how often I get asked that question at the beginning of my first visits."

We felt ridiculous as we laughed it off and moved on quickly to introducing ourselves as we took our seats around the kitchen table.

Taylor spoke with us together and separately about our best attributes and biggest weaknesses.

The questions were tough. They were designed to make us really think about who we were as people. She asked what our families were like growing up. She wanted to know stories about our family vacations and how we did in school. She asked us about our teen years and our biggest regrets in life so far. We had to answer how many kids we planned on having, if we were dealing with fertility issues, and who would watch our future child or children when we were working. Those questions were mentally draining, but then the questions seemed to get even deeper and more difficult to answer.

I remember her asking us how we planned on parenting and disciplining our future child or children. Vince and I looked at each other. We expected this question, but still felt so unprepared for it. We chose honesty, explaining our belief in the fact that every child requires a different approach.

I remember saying something like, "We don't have a perfect answer for you. We feel as if we have an idea of how we want to parent and discipline our child, but until we get to know him or her as a person, it's hard to determine what that will look like. We do not agree with corporal punishment. We hope to have time-outs for the younger years and discussion of consequences to actions for the older years. We want our child to trust us and to know that violence solves nothing. But until we know our child, we don't know exactly what our approach looks like just yet."

Taylor smiled and jotted down a few notes in her notebook. She seemed to understand what we were saying and even mentioned that she agreed, but a small part of me wanted to read her notes over her shoulder just to make sure she wasn't writing down, "No way can these people parent a child."

I kept worrying I was saying all the wrong things. It felt like a test with no right answers. I forced myself to stop wondering about what she wanted to hear and to start focusing on answering honestly.

Once she had us each alone for the one-on-one portion of the visit, she wanted to know what core beliefs we held close to our hearts and our worst fears.

There it was...the moment I choked up and confessed that my biggest fear was losing someone I could not live without. She didn't push further. I'm sure she could tell I was struggling to hold it together, so she moved on after giving me a sympathetic look.

"Okay, next question. What would you say is your favorite thing about Vince?

This one was fairly easy, and I answered without hesitation: "I love how big his heart is. He always tries to do the right thing. He puts everyone else before himself and always wants to make others happy."

Then she asked a tough one: "Ashley, what is your least favorite thing about Vince?"

Wait, what? I just stared at her for a minute while considering my next words. I thought it was a trick question.

I finally answered, "Because of his big heart and desire to help and please others, he can be taken advantage of, which sometimes lends to him holding a lot in and that really is not healthy, but I really have no room to talk. I struggle with the same issue."

Once again, she smiled and wrote in her notebook. I held back the tears once more.

I never did ask Vince what he said in his interview, and he never asked me. It was a moment of self-reflection, almost like a really intense therapy session, if you will.

Taylor called us back together. She asked us to describe the school in our district and the neighborhood. She wanted to know how we planned to incorporate our child's heritage into our family. We explained our desire to learn Japanese together, to discover and celebrate new traditions and cultural practices of Japan, and our hopes to travel back to that beautiful country many times in our future.

We felt as if there could be no further questions...but they continued for the majority of the two-hour session. She inspected our house while taking a break from the interviews, and the highlight of the tour was the nursery we had recently started working on.

Finally, after asking about how we were raised, our favorite hobbies and memories, and what our hopes and dreams were, she said the words I longed to hear:

"I think we're good here. I can get your home study typed up and submitted within the month. I don't need to come back for another visit, one is enough."

We had been told two or three visits were normal, so we felt elated by this. That had to be a good sign!

Vince and I walked her to the door, thanked her multiple times, and said goodbye. Once the social worker was on the other side of our closed door, I let out the breath and the tears I had been holding in. I embraced Stormy and sat on the floor in relief. The first major step in the adoption process was completed. We passed our first test and now we just had to fight...fight for Stormy and fight for ourselves, so we could keep moving forward and stay positive.

Downhill

Unfortunately, the euphoria we felt after the visit came to an abrupt end. Stormy continued to worsen over the upcoming weeks. The remainder of August was consumed with taking him to appointments, doing more research on the best treatment options, and spending as much quality time with him as we could between me coaching cheerleading and Vince coaching golf. When we had a few minutes here and there, we were collecting items for our garage sale fundraiser and also planning a golf outing to help raise additional funds to support our adoption. Being teachers and coaches just added to the stress we were under and made August an exhausting time for us.

> "On Sunday night, August 14, Stormy seemed down and not his normal self. He had just finished his meds and had a vaccine and heart worm pill while at the vet almost two weeks prior. At 3:43 am (the morning of our first teacher workday), he woke me up vomiting. My mom came right over and we rushed him to the emergency vet, while Vince went to school (since we now worked in the same building after Vince took a job at our alma mater) and let everyone know I would not be there until later."

After blood tests, they informed us that Stormy's kidney levels were elevated even more than they had been a couple weeks prior; my heart sank. They said we could come back and see an internist if we would like to do an ultrasound of his kidneys...maybe we could see what was causing the disease progression. We scheduled an appointment and took our boy home with instructions on how to give fluids over the next few days. The goal was to see if his levels would come back down. The idea of sticking him with needles and filling his body with fluids made me feel weak, but if it meant he would feel better, then that's what I would do.

> "Thank goodness Vince's sister is a vet tech and helped us give Stormy his fluids the first three days. We took him back Wednesday night to get his levels rechecked. The kidney levels are coming down, which is good, but two out of three of his liver enzymes are increasing. Luckily, he seems to be feeling better and is acting closer to his old self. I'm hoping he stays that way."

While Vince continued to organize the details of the golf outing and collect items for our garage sale, I devoted myself to spending every spare minute to helping and spending time with my boy.

At the same time, we were also collecting documents needed by our placement and home study agencies. Luckily, many of the forms overlapped, so that saved us a little bit of work. We sent copies of our driver's licenses, social security cards, and passports. We made trips to the County Clerk's Office and the local health department office to collect notarized copies of our birth certificates, marriage license, and immunization records. Vince and I made appointments for wellness checks and asked for copies of all medical records from our family physician. We gathered all pet vaccine records for our cats and dogs as well.

Vince printed off our tax returns from the previous five years and our pay stubs from the three months prior to our home study visit. We asked our boss to write up a reference letter for us, while also using that as proof of employment. Along with our boss, Vince and I asked three other community members and friends to write up reference letters as well.

For us, that was easier said than done. Asking others to write up a letter on our behalf to help us bring home a child somehow felt egotistical or self-gratifying. I know it really isn't, but once again this is an example of how anxiety sometimes takes hold of my way of thinking.

We also typed up a short autobiography, writing about our childhoods and defining moments, as well as our relationship. We had to document the reason for choosing to adopt in general, along with why we chose international, and more specifically, Japan. I felt as if I was interviewing for a job as a parent, which I guess is exactly what we were doing.

It's difficult to describe this paperwork process to someone who has not gone through it. Have you ever applied for a mortgage before? Well, it's not really like that at all, because the adoption paperwork and process is much more detailed and complicated. With a mortgage, all the lender cares about is whether you can afford and care for the home. With adoption, it's about whether you are fit to raise a human being. How do you put that on paper?

Not only did Vince and I complete initial application forms for both our placement and home study agencies in May and July, but we were now also filling out pages of immigration forms to send to USCIS, staying up late into the night on many occasions. I'm a night owl by nature, but Vince was downing the coffee in order to keep up.

I giggle when I think back to one night specifically. It was past midnight, and I was going strong. Vince was on his third cup of coffee, but it was no longer having any effect. He was snoring with his head on the table while I finished the last signature on the form I was on.

"And we're done!" I proclaimed.

Well, I must have been louder than I thought because he jerked awake and replied, "Yep! What did we finish?"

I chuckled and explained that I had completed the final immigration form so we could mail them out the next morning. He scribbled his final signature on the last page as well and then stumbled off to bed.

Collecting the paperwork and filling out never-ending forms was a grueling task, but we were also trying to raise money by spending weekends putting on fundraisers. The last two weekends in August, we held the golf outing, where we made approximately $3,000 and the garage sale, where we profited about $360.

It was all such a crazy experience for me. I was excited to be moving forward in the adoption journey, but still completely broken inside about Stormy's condition.

> "We were fingerprinted on Tuesday, August 16, and our agency sent us our I-600A immigration form as well. We just finished our fire inspection today and made copies of our birth certificates and marriage certificate for both agencies. Now all that's left is to mail the last of the home study forms to our home study agency and the I-600A form and copies of certificates to our placement agency.
>
> Along with that, we owe the government $850 to process the

immigration form, our placement agency $8,750 for the first fees, and $750 to our home study agency. Of course we are also having to pay for Stormy's medical expenses on top of this. Once we get the fees paid, and the home study approval, we wait for our immigration form to be approved. Then we are on the list to await a referral."

By the first week of September, we had finally submitted all documents, letters of recommendation, and our autobiographical statements. That was also the week we took Stormy in to have an ultrasound on his kidneys. The internist was amazing, but of course his job was to be honest. He explained to us that Stormy was unable to absorb the protein from foods properly, and it was causing irreparable damage to his kidneys. He also had extremely high blood pressure, which was damaging the kidneys as well.

I knew there was more to it than that. I could just feel it. From the research I had been conducting, I felt confident he had another condition. The internist agreed that he might have something called Cushing's Disease as well, because he did find what he assumed was a benign tumor on his adrenal gland, and we could test for it, but the test was pretty extensive.

Cushing's could be treated somewhat and this could give Stormy more time, though. I clung to the hope in that sentence. It was the first hopeful piece of advice I had heard.

We conducted the test a few days later, and it came back positive for Cushing's, but it was still in the early stages. We started him on medicine to help treat it, but like everything else, it was trial and error. I left that day feeling a little more hopeful than I had felt in over a month.

The very next day, we started his new medication and took him for the first time to the new holistic veterinarian. She was amazing with him, and the acupuncture seemed to help him feel better. We also decided on some Chinese herbs that would help his kidneys and inflammation. She gave me her cell phone number and personal email address so I could contact her any time. We planned on taking him in once or twice a month for acupuncture. I felt a true peace when I was with her. It's difficult to explain, but for the first time in over seven weeks, I could breathe. We went home and had a great couple of days.

But things turned south again. After two good days, Stormy was slowing down again, and when I came home from work on day three, he was unable to get up off the floor and had zero energy. We rushed him to the emergency vet office once again, where we were told the Cushing's medicine was too strong and had pushed him too far the other way.

I crumbled to the floor right there in the office and just cried. I felt so hopeless and completely defeated. I felt I had done this to him. The internist said we needed to treat him by putting him on a steroid for a month, and then we could put him back on a lower dose of the current medication. For the rest of September and part of October we were focused on getting Stormy's medicine figured out and taking him to see our holistic veterinarian for acupuncture.

At the same time, we were trying to make as many memories as we could. We took him on very slow walks every other night, laid out in the backyard enjoying the breeze and the stars, and went on adventures, such as getting ice cream and going on long drives. We took him and Jackie, our Jack Russell Terrier, on a hike one day in October when he was feeling wonderful. It will always be one of my favorite memories of that fall. We took photos in the sunflower field, and those photos are some of my most treasured memories.

By the end of October, Stormy was feeling pretty well overall, we were officially home study-approved, we had raised over $7,000 for our adoption...but we had over $5,000 in

Pictures in the sunflower fields

32

debt for Stormy's veterinarian bills. We had not planned on this added debt, but it didn't matter. I would have sold everything I owned and given every last penny if it meant my boy would be okay. Yes, I do understand how drastic that sounds, but I vowed to him and myself that he would be given every opportunity to have a long, healthy life.

So the $7,000 went into our adoption savings account, and we put every emergency vet bill on our credit card. This wasn't ideal, but we were determined to make it work somehow. To say I was stressed out and exhausted would be the understatement of the year, but I knew I had to stay strong, not only for Stormy, but also for our future little one.

November was going to be a big month for us because we were about to send in that first big payment of $10,350 to our placement agency so that our I-600A paperwork could be submitted to USCIS. We knew that it could take forty-five to ninety days to be approved, so our hope was to have the approval by the end of the year. We just had to find a way to get the additional $3,000 so we could submit our first big payment to our agency and get the paperwork mailed in.

We still have no words adequate enough to express how thankful we were and still are for those who lovingly helped us reach that goal right before the end of October. We had a rather large donation from someone Vince knows through coaching golf and we held two other small fundraisers, which pushed us over our goal. The outpouring of love and support and generosity of others is what amazes me even to this day.

> "Everyone says to us, 'I bet you can't wait to bring that baby home!' In a way, those people are correct, but to be completely honest, we are enjoying the journey. Every single day is a blessing, so yes, we can wait.
>
> Not because we don't want our baby home, because of course we do, but because we don't want to take one single day for granted. Yes, we can wait because we are enjoying the ride."

"Enjoying the ride." I look at those words now and realize I was desperately trying to stay hopeful during that time. I felt this was God and the universe teaching us a lesson in control, humility, and faith.

I won't lie...I was also angry and felt betrayed. How could a couple who took a giant leap of faith be punished at the one time they desperately needed a reprieve? We already weren't sure how we were going to afford all the adoption expenses to begin with, and then we suddenly had all of Stormy's unexpected medical expenses added on. We were anxious about the adoption process, and now had to deal with even more anxiety piled on over the thought of losing our boy.

We wanted nothing more than to be excited and happy, but then had to figure out how to balance those feelings with the overwhelming sadness of Stormy's illness. It was a never-ending internal battle over which emotion would take control at any given moment. I felt like a pawn in the board game of life and I kept drawing the cards everyone tries to avoid.

The next card would be yet another game-changer. Good thing I put my seatbelt on, because I never saw the next bend in the road coming. I mean, at this point, it would have just been unnecessarily cruel to throw us another curveball, right?

CHAPTER 3

Learning to Grieve, Learning to Cope

Admitting that my biggest, deepest fear was, and still is, losing someone I cannot live without, opened a floodgate of stress and anxiety for me. It was as if saying those words out loud gave them power over me. The fear of losing a member of my family or Stormy kept me awake at night.

I have been fortunate that death was something I rarely had to face as a child. Actually, the first time I lost someone I was truly close to was when I was in college. I lost my great-grandpa, who we all affectionately called Granddad. It was difficult to handle, but I also knew how lucky I was to have had him in my life for as long as I did.

Then, shortly before turning thirty, I lost both of my dad's parents and one of his brothers in a span of eighteen months. The more deaths I experienced, the worse my anxiety became. I realized that the people I loved were aging and death is, of course, inevitable for all of us. I began to cling to those around me and worry over them endlessly. I honestly was unsure how I would survive losing someone else I loved.

It felt as if my fears had manifested into reality. While trying to contain my anxiety over Stormy's illness, along with the stress of the adoption paperwork and process, I received more devastating news one day in early October.

"Ashley," my mom said, "so you know Papaw has been getting some testing done, right?"

My breathing became labored and my head began spinning as I sat down on the chair across from my mom. It was hard to breathe, as if I had just finished running five miles and my lungs just could not take in enough air. I knew where this conversation was headed. She could barely look me in the eyes.

"He has lung cancer," she continued, "and it's pretty bad. He is starting an experimental drug because he refuses chemo and radiation."

I had no words. I just remember crying. My mom knew how difficult this news was for me to hear. My family is not very good at showing sadness or weakness, and we hate to be pitied, so she left me alone to try to process the news she had just given me.

I am ashamed with how I dealt with my grandpa's cancer. I avoided it. I pretended it wasn't happening. I didn't know how to process my emotions. He was my last living grandfather and I was crushed thinking he might not survive this. So for me — and I get this from my mom as well — I ignored it. Ignoring and burying my head in the sand is how I made it through the month of October. I am not proud of my coping mechanism, but I'm working on it still to this day.

Vince was much better at facing the cancer diagnosis. He had gone through it with his dad, and his uncle had just been diagnosed with cancer the year before as well. We were maintaining our appearance of being hopeful and excited on the outside, but struggling behind closed doors to come to terms with two cancer diagnoses, along with Stormy's illness.

November arrived...national adoption month. How appropriate it was that November was the month when Stormy felt a little better, we were completely home study-approved, and we finally submitted our I-600A form to USCIS. We received an email from our placement agency the day before Thanksgiving stating they had mailed our forms to the government and that we should hear something within forty-five to ninety days. That was something to be thankful for. The wait was going to be excruciating, but we were really focused on making every day count and not wishing the days away.

We were also thankful my grandpa was still with us trying to fight the cancer. It was taking its toll on him, though, along with the entire family. We could all see the new medicine did not seem to be helping much, and we were all trying to come to terms with it in our own way. Me, still trying to avoid it; one of my cousins was very rational about it and thought of it as a part of life while also being horribly sad; and another cousin assumed the role of caretaker since she was headed to nursing school, helping my grandma.

Meanwhile, Stormy was feeling great the entire month of November, which was also something to be thankful for. It made my heart happy to see him barking at thunderstorms and chasing birds outside. The fear of losing him was still there, but some days, I took a step back and just thanked God for the good pieces of life.

The pain of the unknown and the adoption wait was still there too, but I covered it up most days the best I could. I tried harder than ever to smile through the pain on the bad days, but at times, I shattered and sat on the bottom of my shower sobbing uncontrollably as my grief took control of every part of me. Those days were scary because I was unsure of how much more I could possibly take.

Vince was so incredibly strong. He's a fixer, remember? He wanted to make things better, but he knew the circumstances we were struggling with were out of his control. With all these illnesses, I felt as if the world was against us, but he tried so hard to make me smile and stay positive. This adoption journey should have been one of the happiest moments of our lives, but we were saddled with guilt because we just could not stay excited and happy while our world crumbled around us.

At the beginning, everything is a rush to get paperwork turned in. Then you wait. You wait for the government to approve you, you wait for a referral, and in some cases, you wait to travel. November was also a month of waiting on the adoption front. We had completed all the paperwork we could and were now just waiting to hear back from USCIS.

The wait was tough as it gave me more time to focus on my grandpa, Vince's uncle, and Stormy. So I was very thankful for fate allowing me to connect to some pretty amazing families going through the adoption process the same time as we were, especially an amazing woman named Tomomi.

On November 18, I received an email from Tomomi asking about our adoption agency and our thoughts on the process so far. I reached out and we emailed back and forth for weeks before ultimately connecting on social media. What did people do before social media?

Tomomi's father is Japanese and her mother is American. She has a wonderful husband and the cutest son and was hoping to adopt from Japan. She had just joined the program and we ended up staying connected and formed a priceless and valuable bond helping each other through some amazing and scary times. We cried when the other felt pain and we celebrated when either of us had good news to share.

I owe more than I could ever express in words to Tomomi...especially the many times she talked me off the ledge. When I was having a bad day because of the illnesses of Stormy or my grandpa, or the adoption wait, she always had words that could speak right to my soul. Nobody, even close family and friends, could calm me down like she could. When I spoke about Stormy as if he were true family, she never judged me. As an animal lover and activist herself, she completely understood me in a way I felt nobody else could. She could make me laugh and cry in the same conversation. Tomomi has a way of saying things so bluntly, but not at all harshly. She might actually be my idol...she really is just one of the coolest humans I know. I am beyond thankful that this journey and our placement agency brought us together.

Thanksgiving was spent being thankful for what we had and for the good in our lives. Unfortunately, a few days later, Stormy hurt his ankle while playing in our backyard. I was incredibly grateful Stormy felt well enough to play, but of course I blamed myself for yet another injury he had to overcome.

Once again, Vince and I took Stormy to the vet and had his ankle examined. After taking x-rays, the doctor noticed bone deterioration, which could signify arthritis or Osteoporosis, a bone infection...or bone cancer.

There it was.

The word I dreaded more than anything was spoken aloud. Cancer.

Again, I felt numb. I was beginning to get used to this feeling. It was as if my body had no way of processing the words spoken, so it just shut down in an attempt to protect itself. I instantly thought about Papaw Bud and Vince's uncle Todd fighting this horrible disease, and I knew I could not take another cancer diagnosis.

We ultimately decided not to do a biopsy since he would need to be sedated, which would make it a high-risk procedure with his kidneys being so weak. If it turned out to be cancer, the only option would be to amputate, and that would have also been detrimental to his overall health. We held tightly to the hope that it was just arthritis since he was nearing ten years old and had shown signs before.

Instead, we took him more often to see Dr. Jo, our holistic veterinarian, and I truly believe the acupuncture and herbs helped him more at that point than any modern medicine could have. For the next several weeks leading up to Christmas, I picked him up and carried him out to potty and continued showering him with love and attention.

November ended, and before we knew it, December and the Christmas season was upon us. My only prayers were that we would hear some kind of good news before Christmas...whether it was on the adoption front, or that Stormy would be healed of at least his ankle issues, or that all our family members would still be with us.

Believe it or not, all three prayers were answered by Christmas Day.

Family photo with Stormy (Left) and Jackie (Right)

We received a letter only ten days after Thanksgiving with an appointment date and time to get our fingerprints taken (yet again) at the immigration office so that our I-600A form could be approved: December 19, right before Christmas break from school would begin.

I remember walking into the immigration office in a nearby city, feeling out of place and not at all comfortable. We walked in and informed the not-so-pleasant woman at the front desk why we were there. Her response floored me.

"Oh, another couple thinking they can save the world by adopting overseas instead of from right here in America."

Vince and I were knocked completely speechless. We had been preparing for situations like this, but had not yet really had anything remotely this hateful said to us, so we had lost all ability to form a coherent reply. We just pretended not to hear her and waited for her to tell us where to wait.

"Okay," she said. "Take a seat over there and someone will assist you."

Vince and I walked to the hard plastic chairs next to a couple of men from Mexico who were immigrating to Ohio.

I remember sarcastically telling Vince, "Well, she was lovely."

"Yeah, just peachy," he replied. "I wonder if she's lucky enough to have that disposition all the time, or if she reserves it for work only."

We both chuckled quietly and then sat in silence waiting for our turn to get our fingerprints and photos taken so our immigration form could be approved.

Vince and I were called over to a little booth where another woman waited with a look of complete disgust. I smiled brightly and said hello. She did not return the kind sentiments. Instead, she ordered me to place my fingers on the electronic device so they could obtain my prints. I was a nervous wreck when one of my prints didn't come through correctly.

"Try it again," she huffed in exasperation

I placed my pinky finger back on the screen and maneuvered it until it worked. Once completed, she pointed to the next booth.

"I go there next?" I asked innocently.

The woman sighed heavily and nodded. I quickly moved away from her station and wished Vince luck as he became her next victim.

The man at the next booth seemed a little more approachable, so I smiled and once again offered him a polite hello. In his defense, he at least smiled back, but did not respond. I decided I was done being friendly.

He told me to sit in the chair so he could take my photo for the immigration paperwork. I sat down and instinctively smiled. That was a big mistake...

"What are you doing?" he asked me harshly.

"I-I don't know. What am I supposed to do?"

"Not smile. They like to see your face without a smile so they can see your features better."

"Okay. My bad," I answered.

Wiping the smile off my face was not hard after the mood I was now in from dealing with these people. After an acceptable photo was achieved, I moved out of the way while Vince came to get his picture. I whispered to him, "Don't smile."

As he sat down, the man yelled at me to leave the booth, so I walked to the waiting area while Vince finished up. I was almost in tears. I hated being treated with so much animosity and disrespect.

When Vince joined me, he noticed my wet eyes and knew that I was holding back tears. I asked him if we were allowed to leave and he wasn't sure. He decided to go ask the lady at the front desk, thankful that it was a different woman than when we had arrived.

When he came back, he said, "All good. Let's get out of here."

I asked him what had taken so long, and he smiled as he explained that he let this new lady, who happened to be the supervisor, know how disrespectful all three people were to us. She said she would take care of it.

When I looked back after walking out the door, I noticed all three people were with the supervisor, and by the way she was pointing and moving her hands, it seemed as if she was letting them know about how wrong it was to treat us like they did. I felt vindicated.

On the way home, I recall Vince and I discussing how we needed to handle those types of people, people who did not understand or agree with us adopting internationally. Everyone is entitled to their own opinion, but people are not entitled to treat others with such disrespect. But by the time we arrived back at school to finish out the day, we had still not come up with any real responses to people that spoke out loudly against our decision. It was something we planned to work on over the next several weeks.

Christmas was almost upon us, which is one of my favorite times of year. I love the happiness and joy people feel. It is the only time I love the cold weather and the hope of snow. I adore the music playing in every store. I love the lights and the Christmas trees, and my favorite part is buying gifts for people. I usually start thinking about Christmas presents in June so I can always come up with meaningful gifts. I absolutely love it.

I reached down deep that year to find some happiness and joy. I wanted desperately to feel like I always do at Christmas, but it was much harder in 2016.

Stormy was walking better and feeling great the day before Christmas Eve, which was a miracle in and of itself. I was happy and thankful for that. And all of our family members were still with us...but barely.

Unfortunately, my grandpa was doing poorly. Nobody expected him to hold on much longer, and once again, I felt broken. This constant brokenness was beginning to feel like my new normal.

It was the strangest feeling. I was so excited that our I-600A approval was moving faster than expected and felt almost giddy at the fact that Stormy felt so well, but I also felt so helpless watching one of the toughest men I have ever known waste away in front of me. I could hardly stand to see him that way.

Dancing with Papaw Bud at my wedding.

I'll never forget the words my grandpa spoke to me just the summer before. He was working out in extreme heat one day while I was enjoying their pool. I told him to go inside and take a break before he had a stroke in the heat. His reply back was exactly what I expected to hear:

"Kid, I'm too damn mean to die. Don't worry about your grandpa."

I chuckled and he laughed that boisterous laugh of his as he continued working on that lawn he was so proud of. I will never forget that laugh — I can still hear it when I think about him.

My heart broke on Christmas Eve when we went to visit him in the hospital. The experimental drug had actually done the opposite of what it was intended to do. He was in the small percentage of people (less than 10% to be exact) that the drug actually attacks the body instead of the cancer. There was nothing else any doctor could do.

Papaw Bud was my last living grandpa and the one I had always been closest to, but he did not even resemble the man I had known my entire life. I barely recognized him. My breath hitched and my heart hurt knowing he wasn't going to be with us much longer.

That night was the last night I saw him. I couldn't bear to go back. He wasn't there, not really anyway. Before we left, I whispered to him how much I loved him and always would. I walked out as the tears fell silently down my cheeks and never looked back.

I'm not sure there are words to convey the way I felt during those months...I just did not know how to handle all the pain I was feeling. I was overwhelmed, terrified, angrier than ever before, and utterly devastated.

That night was the first night since we started the adoption process that I did not pray. Instead, I silently yelled at God. I had never known such pain, and I had no idea how to fully process it. I became angrier and angrier. And as ashamed as I am to admit this, that was the last time I talked to God for months.

I tried to make Christmas Day as happy as I could because I knew deep in my heart this might be Stormy's and definitely would be Papaw Bud's last Christmas, but it just wasn't the same. I was an actor playing a part... I said the right words and smiled at all the right times, but I don't think anyone believed me. I just could not cover up the sadness in my eyes.

When grief weighs you down, and when anxiety creeps up the back of your neck and threatens to strangle you, it's hard to be anything except angry and resentful. Pretending to be happy was getting harder and harder. The only way I can explain it is to say I felt as if I was drowning in the middle of the ocean. My lungs burned as they struggled to suck in air. My arms were flailing, looking for anything to hold on to. My heart was beating hard and fast in my chest. And the worst part was that my head was begging for the chance to let go and enjoy the darkness.

I was so tired of fighting to be happy, but a part of me knew there was still happiness to be had. I just had to get out of the ocean of despair threatening to drag me under.

2017 is Here[5]

> "Well, it is officially 2017... In a matter of a few, short weeks, we have received great news on the adoption front and have lost someone very dear to both of us. We are both physically, emotionally, and mentally exhausted, but moving forward as life intended.
>
> I made a small New Year's resolution this year, and I am already failing. I swore I would try to make my blog posts more uplifting since we have been real downers lately. My goal is not to depress anyone, but to inspire you all. Unfortunately, this post will still be a little on the depressing side, but isn't that how life works sometimes?
>
> First off, as mentioned in previous posts, Vince and I have a few people close to us battling cancer and other issues. My last living grandpa, Papaw Bud, passed away after a very brief battle with cancer on January 6. Our entire family is feeling the loss deeply. He was definitely larger than life and has left behind a huge gaping hole that will never be filled.
>
> He was ornery and feisty, so it is hard imagining him gone, but he

---

[5] Our blog post from January 15, 2017.

45

had one soft spot...his six grandkids. He loved us fiercely and was always proud of us, even when we may not have deserved it. Vince also became very close with him over the years and even considered him a grandpa of his very own. He spent most weekends golfing with him and my two uncles. So he is feeling the loss deeply as well.

Putting on a brave face and dragging myself to school and to the games with my cheerleaders is exhausting. I know it needs to be done, but more than anything, I would love to be spending time with my grandma, who was married to him for fifty-seven years, and the rest of my family. Unfortunately, I have responsibilities and I have tried my best to keep up with them all. I'm trying to be enough for everyone."

I remember feeling inadequate during the entire adoption process, but especially after losing my grandpa. I was still expected to teach and coach. I was still caring for Stormy and taking him to appointments. And I was still trying to be fully present during the adoption journey. I was being pulled in so many directions — trying to be upbeat about the adoption while also grieving the loss of one of my favorite people.

I was not fully present for anything. Nobody was getting my full attention. My cheerleaders, my students, my family and friends all got a part of me, a shell of who I could have been. I kept trying to be what I expected myself to be, but I never truly gave myself any grace, or a chance to grieve completely. I kept myself busy, but what I think I truly needed was a chance to slow down.

"My cousins and I were reminiscing at his memorial service...We laughed, we cried, and through it all, we were wishing Papaw could have been there to hear us. He would have loved that. I know my words are not doing my feelings justice...but I have no words for how much I love my family and how greatly Papaw will be missed.

Time flies by in the blink of an eye...I am so thankful that I have always cherished every second spent with my family, pups, and friends, and I pray that I can continue to take it all in. Because one day, all we will have left are the memories and the pictures.

Now for the more uplifting news. (I need a break from the other...my throat is burning from the raw emotion and tears I'm struggling to hold back.) We spoke with Kelsey, the assistant director from our placement agency, the first week of January. We have received our final approval letters from USCIS and received an email from the US Embassy in Tokyo saying they are expecting our arrival and are hoping to make everything as easy and enjoyable as possible while we are in Japan.

The last piece we need is an email from the US Visa Department releasing our visa number for our son or daughter. Once that comes in, which should have happened last week, we are officially on the list. But she let us know that since we are so close, she can tell us we will be third on the American list! There is also a Canadian list. The three ladies in Japan that are due in January have babies that will be going to Canada because they do not fit the US description of an orphan.[6] But our agency informed us that we could have a referral within the next two months. WOW!

We are praying that we will have our son or daughter home before Easter, which is thirteen weeks from today. Not only do we hope this for us and for our future child, but also for my entire family.

Another positive event to tell is that Stormy has been feeling great since about the week before Christmas. Thank goodness. His kidney and liver levels are still high, but not as high as they were in November and he seems to be feeling like his old

---

[6] For the US to consider a child from another country an orphan, the child must fit one of two categories: either both parents are deceased or have abandoned the child. Or there is only one parent and that parent cannot raise the child due to financial reasons or medical reasons, and the sole surviving parent must irrevocably relinquish rights to the child.

self...almost."

I was questioning everything that we were going through, wondering if things would continue to get worse or finally start to get better. The next couple months would be misleading, to say the least.

> "One final thought...sometimes I find myself wondering why so many things in our lives started to go wrong after starting the adoption process. I even had to ask myself if maybe it was a sign that we shouldn't have gone through with it. That thought left my head pretty quickly though. I begged and pleaded with God to let Stormy and my grandpa get better and to allow them both to be here when we brought our little one home. Obviously, God had other plans and took my grandpa home. In the last week, I have come to terms with that to an extent.
>
> I have also found myself wondering if God held off on opening the Japan program until this year because He knew I would need this adoption to help get me through losing my grandpa and dealing with Stormy's illnesses. I'm not going to lie, the one thing (besides my family and friends) keeping me sane, keeping me going, keeping me from breaking and falling completely apart is this adoption. Maybe the timing isn't wrong like I have been thinking...maybe it's exactly right."

With that, I slowly began allowing hope to creep inside me. Then the universe ripped that hope right out from under me and left me breathless all over again.

CHAPTER 4

Emotional Whiplash

After losing the patriarch of my mom's family on January 6, 2017, I felt the familiar feeling of numbness. At the time, I had no words for the way I was feeling, but now, looking back, I realize I was protecting myself by not allowing myself to feel the true extent of the pain. Everyone processes grief differently, and I have never been good at it (whatever that means). One minute, I was struggling to catch my breath, and the next, I was daydreaming about my future little one. It was emotional whiplash.

My anxiety punished me for feeling any kind of joy and hurled me into the dark abyss of guilt and grief over the realization that my grandpa, one of my favorite people, would never meet his future great-grandchild. It was exhausting, and in an attempt to protect myself, I shut down. I did not want to feel anything, because I knew the moment I allowed myself to feel, I would break, and I did not have time to break...

I had Stormy to take care of, adoption paperwork to finish, cheerleaders to coach, and students to teach. My grief was locked up in a dark room inside myself, and I threw away the key. I didn't want to face it, or feel it, or deal with it in any way. Looking back, I know how unhealthy that was. The only way to get to the other side of the storm...is to weather it.

While struggling to hide the extent of my pain, my anxiety forced me to believe everyone who asked me how I was doing, was truly asking me if I was still holding it together. I interpreted every look they gave me as pity. I hated it, but in my mind, everyone was wondering when I was going to snap emotionally, mentally, and physically.

My relationships struggled and I was lashing out without even recognizing what I was doing. I smiled and said I was fine when people asked, while the grief locked away inside screamed to be let out and the anxiety lied by telling me people felt sorry for me and knew I was one bad day away from breaking.

After saying I was fine, I would change the subject and discuss the adoption or how hard my cheerleaders were working toward our regional and state competitions. The change of subject worked well, because let's be honest and just say it...nobody really feels comfortable discussing grief and death. People were just as relieved as I was when the subject was changed.

As I was working on keeping the overwhelming sadness at bay, good news was emailed to us on January 20. We were finished with paperwork and on the official waiting list for a beautiful baby from Japan. It felt (for so long) as if that day was never going to arrive, and then, in what seemed like a blink of an eye, it was here in the form of an email that read:

"There are still just two paper-ready families ahead of you, so #3!"

I reread the email a few times. Not only were we on the list, but Kelsey was giving us the thrilling news that there were only two families ahead of us.

Vince and I wanted to announce it to the world. We called and texted family and friends almost immediately, and they celebrated with us and rejoiced over the good news. It had been a tough month, and this was a major step in our journey, so we felt as if we had won a gold medal in this marathon called adoption.

I remember telling my grandma in person. I was nervous because I knew, like me, she would be thinking about how Papaw Bud missed meeting his first great-grandchild by possibly just a few short months.

"Mamaw," I began one day at the end of January when Vince and I were visiting her, "we have good news on the adoption front. We are officially on the list and there are only two families in front of us!"

She smiled so big and replied, "Oh, that is such good news! And Lord knows we need some good news around here for a change."

I have always admired my grandma. She was a pillar of strength after losing my grandpa, her high school sweetheart and the only man she ever loved. I never saw her shed a tear, let alone break down. I tried so hard to be as strong as her. Now that I am removed from those times, I am positive she had her moments, most likely behind closed doors. I come from a long line of "closet criers," my term for those of us who refuse to show sadness in front of others. We bottle it up until we are behind closed doors, where we feel safe enough to let the tears fall.

February began and Vince and I were busier than ever, which was a blessing and a curse. It is harder to fall into the black hole of grief and despair when you have other aspects of your life demanding your attention. I was preparing my cheerleaders for a regional cheer competition and Vince was helping coach the boys basketball team. We were working on setting up the nursery, and I was trying hard not to buy every cute baby outfit I saw.

Many women talk about the idea of "nesting" when they are expecting a baby. Adopting a child is no different. Now that we knew we were getting closer and closer to bringing home a baby, my instincts were kicking in. We had already been working on the nursery, but now I was insisting on every tiny detail being perfect.

In the fall, we had bought the furniture and had a friend paint a cute giraffe, tree, and elephant on the walls. But now, we were placing books on shelves, filling baskets with diapers and other necessities, putting up shelves, and washing and hanging up baby clothes. We were cleaning

Finishing touches on the nursery.

everything in sight and decluttering even more than what we did before our home study visits. I never really believed in the idea of nesting, but man, was it real! It was this strange urge to feel ready for our little one.

Vince and I were also saving literally every single penny. I had been collecting change from everywhere...my pockets, Vince's pockets, our couch, our cars, the sidewalk, fountains, wherever. Okay, I didn't actually take coins out of fountains, but I may or may not have considered it.

It was incredible to see how quickly change could add up just one coin at a time. In a way, it was therapeutic and strangely calming knowing that something as small as a penny made a world of difference. In fact, by the time our journey ended and we traveled to Tokyo, we had saved over three hundred dollars just from the change.

On February 2, just one day shy of two weeks, we opened an email to read:

"I am excited to inform you that you are now second on the American list!"

We read the email multiple times because we could not believe it. How were we number two on the list already?!

The program was moving faster than ever and four families welcomed little ones home from Japan that January. This was unprecedented in this small program. We were shocked and thrilled — but also slightly panicked at the thought that we could be bringing home our baby in a few short weeks.

I remember looking at Vince, slightly panicky, and saying, "Holy cow. It's really happening. We could bring a baby home within a month or two!"

Vince smiled and said, "I'm kind of freaked out. How about you?"

"Yep! Yes, I am."

We laughed anxiously and then fell into an uneasy silence, both of us thinking about our future and trying hard not to be terrified at the thought of being responsible for a tiny human.

We kept up the penny-pinching more than ever and worked on preparing ourselves mentally and emotionally for our new little blessing. We also spent days relaxing, since we felt that once the baby came home, we would end up being sleep-deprived and overwhelmed with stressful parenting decisions. This was our chance to relax and prepare ourselves for a whole new lifestyle.

On February 20, exactly one month after officially being placed on the waiting list, the temperature reached sixty degrees and the sun was shining brightly. Sixty degree days in February in Ohio are rare. I remember this day clearly because Stormy was soaking up the sun and feeling great. Like most Shelties, he loved the snow and cold weather, but because of his Cushing's Disease, he was losing hair and could not regulate his body temperature well, so he was having to wear a coat all winter long. It broke my heart seeing him shiver while trying to roll and play in the snow, which had always been his favorite thing to do.

It was a Sunday and Vince and I decided we needed to decompress. One of the ways I like to relax and relieve anxiety is to get out in nature and walk. So we took Stormy and Jackie and we walked around our neighborhood. We didn't discuss finances or the nursery or traveling to Japan or Stormy's illness. Instead, we enjoyed the sun and each other and the time with our pups, soaking in the moment. I felt as if that was the first time I had taken a moment to catch my breath since July of the year before. It felt wonderful to breathe and feel a small amount of hope creep its way into my heart.

As February came to a close, we had not heard from our agency and we were curious as to whether or not the family who was number one on the list had gotten a referral. In a practice of patience, I forced myself to wait to email. Kelsey at the agency was on maternity leave and I really did not want to burden the others in the office who were working hard in her absence.

I planned on emailing our agency on March 1, but on February 27, the email we had been waiting on came from Kelsey who was apparently working at home while on maternity leave. I frantically opened the email and breathlessly read the words we had been longing to read:

"Just wanted to let you know that the family ahead of you received their referral of a baby girl today!"

We were officially number one on the list and were told the next potential US-bound baby was due on March 28...just one month away. After months of waiting and time creeping by, it now felt as if we were racing to the finish line. It's surreal knowing you could receive an email or phone call at any moment that will change your life forever. Vince and I were just one phone call away from the rest of our lives.

As we were preparing for a referral, I had an amazing friend from high school reach out to me about a baby shower. We had remained friends through the years, but we both led busy lives and had drifted apart. We had reconnected as I followed her family's adoption journey of bringing home two sweet children from the Democratic Republic of the Congo.

By February of 2017, both of their kids were home and she decided to open her home to my family and friends in order to host a baby shower for me. I was blown away by her generosity and brought to tears when she volunteered to host. I hadn't actually given much thought to a shower since we were unsure of whether we would be matched with a boy or a girl. And to be honest, I wasn't sure how a baby shower worked for families adopting.

That's a strange statement, I know, but the process and experience of adopting a child are completely different than having a biological child. I wasn't sure if a shower would happen. But a few of my dearest friends decided that now that we were number one on the list, a baby shower

Showered with gifts

was exactly what we needed. So we began planning at the beginning of March.

So when March began, Stormy was still doing as well as could be expected, we were hanging out at number one on the list, and my family and friends were planning me an amazing baby shower for March 19. Overall, life was good.

Stormy celebrated his tenth birthday on March 6, and I was so happy he was still with us and feeling well enough to enjoy a walk and a special birthday treat. I was not too confident that we would get to celebrate another birthday, so we smiled and took photos and enjoyed this bittersweet day to the fullest. I remember smiling for the camera and feeling happy, but looking at those pictures now, I realize my eyes show the real me. I barely recognize myself. I look exhausted and sad, which makes me relive those moments and feelings all over again. But I am so thankful I took those photos with my boy. I will forever cherish every single one.

We finally put the finishing touches on the nursery on March 15 and had baby clothes packed and ready for the call we knew we could get any day.

Staying busy and preparing for the trip helped me stay focused and allowed me a moment away from worrying about life or grieving my grandpa.

On Sunday, March 19, family and friends came out to celebrate our future little one and showered us with gifts. It was a great day spent with close family and friends. I loved and enjoyed every single minute of it and was so excited to tell everyone the latest update we had just received.

We were told the Friday before that they had another mom due March 23, and that could possibly be our little one. They would update us once the baby was born and the mom signed off on the adoption plan. I asked everyone to keep the baby and mom in their prayers. I cannot even fathom the difficulty of the days ahead and decision she was trying to make.

It's an interesting and confusing situation to be in. On one hand, we were praying for peace for our little one's first mom and family, while also hoping and praying this one was our child. My emotions were all over the place. How could I hope that this mom would choose another family to raise her baby? The turmoil she must have been feeling; the decision she had to make for herself and child had to be heartbreaking. This led Vince and me to feel indescribable guilt. How could we feel any excitement while our future child's first momma was making a gut-wrenching and nearly impossible decision?

So instead, I prayed for peace...I prayed that we would feel peace and that the expectant mom would also feel peace, and that we would feel confident in what was meant to be, would be. This was the first time I prayed or spoke to God since Christmas when I went to see my grandpa in the hospital. I felt a deep sense of urgency that I could not explain or comprehend.

I felt this unwavering feeling of uncertainty that literally brought me to my knees. So I prayed hard. I prayed for the moms that were expecting and trying to make the decision that was best for them and their babies. And I prayed for peace for those brave mommas and for us. At the time, I had no idea why I felt such a need to pray, but I did it anyway with an intensity and fierceness I can't explain.

I think I knew deep down that the child that was meant to be ours, would be ours in the end. What I did not know was that the road leading us to our sweet little one would be full of even more twists and turns than we had already experienced. The road we were about to turn onto was not the road we expected. It was a detour.

PART II

The Wait

CHAPTER 5

The Perfect Storm

Spring Has Sprung![7]

"We are still #1 on the US list. We have been in contact with our agency about once a week since the first of March. We have been informed that the program has slowed down a little in the past couple months. I know most might seem frustrated with this news, and we feel the same, but at the same time, we are very thankful.

We are thankful because while things slow down for us on the list, several women on the other side of the world have chosen to overcome the odds and the obstacles stacked against them and raise their little ones. In the months of February and March, ten women at the agency in Japan chose to back out of the program due to deciding to parent, which is actually a wonderful thing.

Another obstacle for us is that many of the birth moms are choosing Canada over the US. I love that the birth mothers have a say in where their little ones go, so this once again does not frustrate us. It gives us peace of mind. Some have asked us why mothers have been choosing Canada over the US. The short answer is that the US requires the birth mother to be interviewed at the US Embassy, and Canada does not have this requirement.

---

[7] Our blog post on our website posted on April 8, 2017.

Some birth moms would rather skip the interview at the Embassy because it makes them feel uncomfortable or sometimes even ashamed, so they sometimes choose Canada for this reason. Either way, it is their choice and we are happy the mothers have this option/choice.

So where does this leave us? Things are possibly speeding up again. There are approximately ten women due between now and the middle of May. From what we have been told, eight of these women, as of now, prefer the US over Canada. We do not know specific due dates, but we feel certain one of these little ones is meant for us. We are praying our little cherry blossom will be coming home sometime in April or May."

Vince and I were officially finished with the paperwork, the nursery, and with getting clothes ready for our future little blessing. March 23 came and went and we were hoping to hear news soon that we had a baby boy or girl waiting for us in Japan. On Friday, March 31, I could not wait any longer and decided to email our agency to see if there was an update.

Our agency was wonderful about responding quickly, so we received a reply within a couple hours informing us that a little one was born, but that his/her momma decided to raise him/her. My heart sank, but also rejoiced for that mom and her baby.

I know some may not fully understand how hopeful adoptive families can be on the journey of adopting but also rejoice when a baby gets to stay with his or her birth family. But think of it this way: we considered ourselves as "the last

A new nursery, just waiting for a baby.

resort." The best case scenario for any child is family preservation, meaning the birth family is the one raising their biological child. In this situation, the baby gets to stay in the country of birth and with his or her birth family.

The next best scenario would be if a family in Japan wanted to adopt, because once again, the baby would stay in the country of birth. We saw ourselves as the next best situation after this. We wanted to give a child a home that had no other option so that the orphanage would not be the end result. This is why my emotions were so complicated...we were waiting eagerly for a child, but also rejoiced when a family was kept together, even if that meant we would be waiting longer.

In that same email, we were told that a baby girl had been born that same day (March 31) and that we should know more by April 4. My heart soared and I felt thrilled at the thought of having a baby girl since my dreams always told me I would have a daughter.

I told myself to not get too excited because this mom could decide on domestic adoption, Canadian adoption, or to raise her baby girl herself. And as mentioned previously, family preservation was the main goal here. But no matter what my head was thinking, my heart was thrilled — and even though I knew it was a bad idea, I went out and bought a few girls items over the weekend.

On April 4, after daydreaming about a beautiful baby girl and picking out potential names, we received an email from our agency saying there was a little mix-up and the baby was actually a boy instead of a girl. I remember reading that email and, I'm ashamed to admit it, but I cried. I so badly had my heart set on a girl.

I had received the email at the end of the school day, so I walked down to Vince's classroom and burst into tears upon entering.

"Whoa! What's wrong?" he asked.

"It's a boy," I answered, unable to hide the disappointment in my voice.

Vince just stared at me in confusion. I explained the email and showed it to him. Our agency was very understanding and even asked us if we would like to hold out for a girl since they had messed up. We knew going into this that we needed to be open to either sex, and I was always okay with that, but something told me we were meant to have a daughter. We felt selfish even considering that option.

To make a long story short — and also because this little one's story is not ours to tell — all I'll say is he did not end up going to a US family at all.

A few days later, on April 11, we were told another baby was born a couple days earlier, also a girl. This time, we were more guarded. It could be a girl, or maybe a boy. This baby once again could be our little one, or maybe not. With adoption, there are so many unknowns, up until bringing your little one home — and even after being home, to be completely honest. This mountain of unknowns can be frightening, especially to someone like me dealing with an undiagnosed anxiety disorder.

The days felt like weeks and hours like days as we awaited more news. The anxiety over becoming a mother in a hotel room on the other side of the world began to sneak in. Like any expectant parent, I began doubting my ability to be a good mom. Not only was I expected to keep a little human alive, which I was fairly confident I could accomplish, but Vince and I had the task of helping this child become strong, independent, caring, kind, confident, empathetic...the list goes on.

I was already having nightmares over the first day of kindergarten, whether our child would be able to make friends, puberty, getting his or her license, how to handle a break up, catching our child sneaking out of the house, graduation...and on and on. The anxiety became a full-grown shadow following me around, ready to pounce the moment any doubt crossed my mind.

Vince and I talked through those fears together and decided we would tackle each issue as they arose. Why was I losing sleep over something years in the future? In a simple answer...anxiety.

Our biggest fears were harder to get a handle on. In today's world of mass shootings, gang violence, lack of respect for human life, and a lack of empathy...how were we going to raise a child to understand that all people should be treated fairly? How could we teach a daughter that bullying and being a mean girl is not okay? How would we teach a son that no means no?

And most importantly, how would we teach our child to understand that everyone is fighting a battle inside and the best way to fight against the evil in the world is to be kind and loving and accepting of everyone? Those thoughts and fears kept me awake at night, especially as the referral moved closer and closer and our little one was closer to being in our arms.

On April 21, we heard that things were still progressing and that the placement agency in Japan had custody of this sweet girl. They were collecting all the documents so they could give us an official referral. At this point, we let ourselves feel hopeful again.

On April 25, we received another email informing us they were awaiting a few more documents and then we would have our referral. At this point, my excitement had increased exponentially, as did my fears and doubts over becoming a mom. This was it!

After reading that email, I remember turning to Vince and saying, "This might really be it. This time, she might be ours."

Vince smiled, cautiously optimistic. He did not want me to get my hopes up just to be let down again.

On April 27, things were still progressing as expected and our agency sent a list of items to remember to bring with us to Japan. It felt so real and we allowed ourselves to get even more excited awaiting the actual referral and, even better, photos of our daughter. For the first time, the excitement began to drown out my fears, and Vince began allowing himself to feel joy as well.

While feeling this excitement, we received news that Stormy's kidney values were elevated slightly more, which brought us down a little. We had backed down on his fluids because of how well he was feeling, and now they were higher than a few weeks before. I hated myself. I felt I had let him down and allowed this to happen. In our blog post that week, I wrote:

> "Stormy went to the vet last Thursday. His BP is great and he lost a pound and a half, which is actually good. He needs to lose about four more since it is better on his joints and heart. The one bad thing is that his kidney levels have gone back up some... So we have upped his fluids and are hoping his levels come back down.
>
> He has also been dealing with some sinus/seasonal allergy stuff (like owner, like pup), which (along with his kidney levels) has him feeling a little blah. So he goes back in on Sunday, April 30. We are hoping and praying he feels better and that his numbers are down some. We fought hard all fall and winter. Now we are almost starting over. It is hard to handle and I feel so guilty."

Then April 28 arrived and we received an email. It was a Friday morning, and we expected the referral that day. We were ecstatic to finally see photos of our daughter. It stated:

"We regret to tell you that baby girl's mom had a change of heart and decided on domestic adoption since there is now a family in Japan interested in adopting."

I felt as if I had been punched in the gut. I could not breathe and felt nauseated. Our hearts broke and our excitement was extinguished instantly.

Vince and I mourned the second daughter we thought we had and then felt guilty at mourning at all. As I have mentioned previously, adoption is hard and confusing. Even though my heart was disappointed, it was also at peace because a domestic family was adopting her. She would get to remain in her beautiful country, and hearing about more families choosing to adopt in Japan made me incredibly happy and hopeful for the future of adoption in Japan.

I vividly remember sitting up most of that night praying hard that Stormy would start to feel better and that we would find our son or daughter soon. I wanted more than anything for Stormy and our little one to meet. I was so confident we had a daughter somewhere and that she was so close to us and within our reach. I held on to that hope all night long until I fell asleep from utter exhaustion.

I had prayed like I had never prayed before...I felt drained and defeated, and then I had this dream. That night I dreamed that we were in Japan meeting our daughter for the first time. It was the most realistic dream I had ever experienced, and I truly felt it was a sign from God. I clung to that dream for the remainder of our wait, but it was incredibly difficult to do.

On April 30, Kelsey was back in the office and we were so thankful to have her contacting us. She always knew the right words to say to comfort us and make us feel hopeful.

On May 3, she informed us that another baby was born and it was also a girl. The agency in Japan was planning on taking custody on May 8 and we would know more after that time. This time, I fought internally with myself any moment I started to feel excited. I refused to believe this was our daughter until we received the official referral. But it was so difficult not to feel those little flutters of anticipation.

I threw all my energy on Stormy by showering him with love and attention. Looking back now, I knew he was starting to slow down, but I kept denying it, lying to myself. I watched him struggle to walk, whether to go potty or around the neighborhood.

But there were times the old Stormy would appear out of nowhere. I still have a video on my phone of him barking and cantering around our backyard. I still watch it every now and then. Apparently, I am a little nostalgic...or maybe it is a way of comforting myself and feeling like he is still here and never forgotten. Sometimes I smile and other times I curl up into a ball and let the grief take over.

Sometimes it's good to feel the grief. Sometimes we need to feel it just so we know we are still alive. I tried so hard to protect myself that I kept all emotions in check. I was going through the motions and playing my role, but inside, my feelings were encased in glass that was threatening to shatter at any minute.

Me and my boy

Vince and I tried to focus on school a lot more too. Sometimes I think back and wish I would have communicated more with Vince about how he felt. I noticed he seemed worn down as well, but I was too caught up in my own feelings to really take on his as well. I know Vince was also struggling with the ups and downs of the adoption process, but he kept saying our time would come and that "what was meant to be, would be." Deep down, I believed him, but a small part of me — the fatalistic part — kept saying, "This is never going to happen for you. You aren't meant to be parents."

My anxiety fueled this little part of me, and it was taking its toll and wearing me down. I kept asking the universe and God why I was put on this path just to be let down over and over again. And then the still somewhat-sane part of me told myself to calm down.

Of course, I was ready to bring a beautiful baby home, but as a person who advocates for all children to have a home, a huge part of me was ecstatic that all these potential little ones found homes in Japan or were part of their loving, biological families.

The adoption process wears on a couple. You really have to be able to communicate, which we did, but looking back, we should have communicated more. For example, I should have explained how anxious I was becoming. I should have described my fears of never getting a referral. I should have asked Vince how he was feeling more. I was just too scared to let my feelings out of their enclosure. It was like opening a dam. Once the emotions started to break through, there would be no stopping them.

When Vince asked me how I was holding up, I said I was disappointed about losing so many possible referrals, but I was doing okay. I kept saying, "I'm fine," but that was a lie. I was not okay. I wasn't fine. Every time we heard we were not receiving a referral, I became more and more anxious that time was running out. I started to think we might never bring home a baby. Also, a big part of me really wanted to see Stormy with our child, and I was afraid I was running out of time to make that happen.

I think the reason the disappointment was too much to take at times, stemmed from the grief and feelings I had not dealt with properly. I did not fully grieve my grandpa, and I was losing Stormy more and more every single day...but I kept trying to hide from the inevitable.

As May progressed, our referral was still supposedly headed our way. I was terrified to admit it at the time, but I was suffering from an anxiety disorder and I was pretty sure depression was sneaking up on me. I was spiraling out of control, and I felt like that was unacceptable. I could not make Stormy better, and I felt like that was unacceptable. I could not fix anything that was happening in our lives, and I felt like that was unacceptable as well.

Meanwhile, Stormy's health was declining. On May 11, he had a wonderful day. He was eating well and drinking and playing. We went for a short walk around our little neighborhood. He was barking at a storm that night and hope kindled inside of me. That was a Thursday, but by Saturday morning, he was refusing food and water and was barely moving. We rushed him to the emergency vet and they gave him extra fluids.

We left and I stayed up all night long, just staring at him and feeling him breathe. I didn't want to miss a single minute with him. Sunday morning, he was not any better.

I remember looking at Vince while holding Stormy on the floor and asking, "Is this it? Is this the day my heart will break and I'll never be the same?"

I think I knew the answer, but I could not face it. Or actually, I refused to face it. We decided to take him back and have the clinic keep him overnight so he could get fluids throughout the entire night.

Looking back now, I regret that decision, because I wish I would have kept him at home where he felt safe and comfortable, and where I could have held him and been with him throughout the night. I was just so desperate to save him that all reasoning and logic left me. I would have literally done anything if it meant he had the chance to live even a few more years.

Stormy was only ten years old, and it just wasn't long enough. To be fair though, forever would not have been long enough. Something about our connection will never be understood by anyone. Even I don't understand it, but it was so real and powerful.

Vince and I didn't sleep much that night. I cried until I had no tears left...the house felt empty without him. We left bright and early for the emergency hospital. As soon as the specialist came into the claustrophobic room, I knew it was not good news. He had the look in his eyes I never wanted to see. The tears flowed down my cheeks as he told us that Stormy took a turn for the worse overnight. I don't think I really processed a single word the doctor said. I just wanted to hold Stormy.

I remember saying, "Please just bring him to me. I just want to see my boy."

As I write this now, years later, I can feel my breath catch, my throat still burning from the raw emotion, and tears fall freely down my cheeks. It hurts too damn much and reliving it is the worst pain I have felt since that day.

68

After Stormy was brought into the small, suffocating room, he laid on my lap. I sat on the cold, hard, uncomfortable floor and stroked his soft fur. I spoke softly to him, kissed him and soaked every second in like it was the air I needed to stay alive.

After twenty minutes of this, I told the doctor to do anything and everything he could to help him. I needed more time. I needed him to meet his sister I was sure would be coming home in a few short weeks. The last words I spoke to Stormy were the words I said to him every night before bed and every day before I left the house. "I love you more than life, boy, and I always will."

I let the tears fall as I watched them take him away. And less than thirty minutes later, they told me he had a heart attack on the table and they could not bring him back. My heart felt like it stopped for a brief moment. I fell to the ground and cried...I cried hard. Vince and I sat with him in the cold, sterile, lifeless room and said goodbye to our boy for almost an hour. I couldn't let them take him away, and I am thankful the hospital gave me all the time we needed.

It's impossible to describe the way I felt. It wasn't that my heart broke or even that it shattered...it felt like it had been completely ripped from my body. I can honestly admit I had not, and still haven't, ever felt pain so deep and so raw in my entire life.

I know part of the grief was for my grandpa. The band-aid had been ripped off and I was feeling all the grief I had been trying to keep locked away over Papaw, the adoption losses, and now Stormy. It had happened...I was changed. In that moment, I knew I would never be the same.

CHAPTER 6

An Ocean of Grief

Grief is like the ocean. You feel in control, the water is hitting your ankles, and when the waves roll in, they hit just at your knees, never higher. You can stay on your feet as long as the water stays below your knees. Then when you least expect it, a wave comes along and knocks you down. You didn't see it coming, you didn't prepare, and now you are on the ground, trying to catch your breath, praying you can get back up on your feet before the next wave hits.

That's how it is for me. I have great days where I think about Stormy and smile, then out of nowhere, a wave of grief hits me and hits me hard. It happens when I am in the shower, and I let myself sink to the floor and cry. It hits me when I am lying in bed trying to fall asleep, and I allow myself to cry silently until exhaustion takes over. And sometimes it hits when I am out running errands, and I force myself to stop and take a deep breath. I push past the tightness in my chest and blink away the sting in my eyes.

I know this may sound like exaggeration, but Stormy was more than a dog to me. He was my best friend, my companion, my boy, and, as Tomomi actually pointed out to me, my soul-dog. Dog people may get

Stormy loved playing in the snow.

that, and some may never understand, but that's okay. After reading up on the term soul-dog and about how some dogs and people have incredible bonds, I knew that described my boy and me.

After prying myself off the floor and walking out the door that day, feeling numb, Vince drove me to my parents' house. I refused to go home. I knew I was not ready to walk through the door and not have Stormy there to greet me like he did every day. I held onto his collar and sat on the couch, crying. I stayed there for five days. I tried going home once to get clothes and had a panic attack after opening the door and realizing he was truly gone.

In my blog post, I chose to put my feelings out there instead of bottling them up like I was so used to doing.

> "One week ago today was Mother's Day...and since then our lives have shifted...it's been one of the worst weeks of our lives and one of the very best...
>
> We thought this would be my first Mother's Day with a human (not just fur) child, but that was not meant to be. On Mother's Day, we took Stormy to the emergency vet and lost our sweet boy on Monday morning after he fought like hell for nine months. There have yet to be words created that are strong enough to describe the unconditional love I feel for him or for the unbearable pain I've felt since losing him. Heartbroken, shattered, destroyed, obliterated, decimated, devastated...none of them even come close to this emptiness I feel or this pain I've felt."

The icing on the cake was that I also had a severe sinus infection at the same time, so I took the whole week off from school. My whole body hurt from grief and from being sick. I couldn't function.

I had so many wonderful friends checking in on me and helping me through one of the worst times of my life. My saving grace was actually Tomomi, though. Our adoption journeys led us to one another, but our love of life and our pups bonded us. I knew she would understand, so I messaged her and she reached out with some of the most insightful, encouraging, inspiring words I have ever had the pleasure of hearing.

> "I do want to thank those of you who have helped me through this week. When the storms rolled through over the last few days, my heart broke all over again...Stormy hated the thunder and would go nuts barking that wonderful Sheltie bark at it for hours. Tomomi told me she honestly believed it was Stormy barking from the sky, letting us know he's okay. That made me smile. I certainly hope so."

Tomomi's words about Stormy barking from the sky is something I have kept close to my heart ever since. I smile every single time I hear thunder, and silently say hi back to my boy.

Besides Tomomi, the only other thing holding me together, at least slightly, was Kelsey and the thought of our baby.

Not Getting Better at the Waiting[8]

> "Well, I actually have no idea how to start this post. So the last three weeks have been the longest of our lives. Up until Stormy's passing, we were really good at the waiting. We didn't mind waiting for a referral because we knew every day that passed was one less day we would have with Stormy. To be honest, I think we all need to slow down and enjoy every single day we get. We rush through life and forget to enjoy it. So we didn't mind the wait at all. But now...now it is getting harder. We are not getting better at the waiting...we are getting worse at it. It is so much harder to deal with and every single day feels like it stretches on and on."

Just four days after losing Stormy, we got a new email from Kelsey...she was beyond thrilled to email us our referral of a beautiful baby girl. It was the first time I smiled all week.

---

[8] Our blog post on our website posted on June 1, 2017.

Vince and I were in love after seeing her beautiful face and reading her first momma's story. I cried tears of joy, and after getting approval from our agency, we shared her face on our social media accounts and decided to go out to dinner with my family to celebrate.

We were showered with love from family and friends. Everyone was over the moon for us. We even named our sweet girl, Everly Sky. Everly was a name we loved and Sky was Stormy's middle name. We wanted a piece of him to be with her forever. Our day finally came, and it could not have come at a better time. I needed something wonderful in our lives, and our baby girl was it.

We started making travel arrangements and booked our hotel at an amazing hotel in Tokyo. We went shopping on Saturday and Sunday and bought everything girly we could find. My mom went crazy and bought ALL the girly things. It was so refreshing being able to go out and not buy gender-neutral items.

We packed our suitcases on Sunday and felt prepared. We also called Adoption Airfare, which is a company that helps find great travel deals for adoptive families, and had them hold tickets for us. We were expected to confirm our visa appointment the next morning, which would allow us to book the tickets. That night, Vince spoke to Kelsey, and the US Embassy confirmed our appointment for the Tuesday after Memorial Day. We were planning on landing in Tokyo in one short week. We could not believe it.

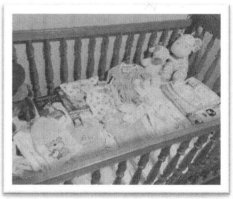

I returned to work Monday morning for the last week of school. The referral came at the perfect time since school would be out, so we would not have to miss work, and we would have the whole summer to bond with our girl. Selfishly, I

Baby clothes packed and ready for our new baby girl.

73

also felt the trip to Japan and bonding with our girl would be the perfect distraction from my grief. I was constantly looking for things to focus on so I wasn't focused on everything I had lost over the last few months.

On Monday, May 22, 2017, I received a phone call from Kelsey during my last period class.

> "Then my phone rang during school, just twenty-five minutes before school let out. I recognized the number as our agency's, so I answered it in the hallway outside of my classroom. Kelsey was on the line in tears. She told me not to book the tickets yet..."

The smile slipped from my face as soon as I heard her voice; I knew this was not good news.

She informed me that our Japanese agency received a voicemail overnight from the baby girl's momma saying she wanted her back. Exactly one week after losing my boy, my whole world stopped turning once again. The girl we had miraculously grown to love in three short days, the girl whose picture Vince had made the background on his phone, the girl we had dreamed about, the girl we thought would be ours...no longer would be.

I couldn't breathe. I had a panic attack similar to the one I had exactly one week earlier. I sat on the cold, hard floor right outside my classroom full of students and listened to Kelsey telling me how sorry she was. Her heart broke right along with mine. Over the last several years, we had grown to become friends. She celebrated when we celebrated and cried when we cried. Before hanging up, she told me she would have more information after the agency met with the mother and discussed everything.

After hanging up, I collected myself the best I could and walked back into the classroom. What felt like hours was actually only three minutes. Luckily, it was the last class of the day and my students were watching the movie that went along with the novel we had just completed in class. I frantically texted Vince to let him know what Kelsey told me. We were supposed to book plane tickets as soon as we got out of school.

Vince was so upset. He was already so connected to this sweet girl, and he felt awful for me. I think he worried that I could not take much more. I was at my breaking point, and I think he wondered how much more I could take before my grip on reality would completely break.

Vince spoke to Kelsey after school.

"Vince, I promise I will call you or email, whichever you prefer, as soon as I hear anything," she said. "Even if it is three in the morning. I am just so terribly sorry this keeps happening to you guys. This has never happened before in the Japan program, and never this many times. I know it is hard to hear right now, but all of this will make sense one day."

Her words calmed Vince and me slightly, but the anxiety could not be completely tamed.

After telling my parents and Vince's mom, we picked up my sister-in-law and best friend, Erica, and headed up to visit one of our other very best friends, Kalyn, in the hospital. The day before, she delivered a healthy beautiful baby girl. We smiled and laughed on the outside, but on the inside, I felt out of sorts. We didn't want to spoil the moment by telling her anything until we knew more details.

When Kalyn spoke about how our girls were less than a month apart and how close they will be as they grow up, we smiled and agreed excitedly. My heart hurt and I was sick to my stomach, but I couldn't bring myself to tell her we may not have a baby girl. Speaking it out loud would make it more real.

Instead I said, "I know! How amazing is it that they will be just a few weeks apart in age and will grow up together?"

After returning home that night, I sat and cried. I could not understand. I felt my daughter. I don't really know how to describe it, but I knew my daughter was out there. I felt her in every single part of my body. So part of me thought maybe this would work out.

At the same time, I was aware of how selfish that thought was. Looking back now, in a clear state of mind, of course it was better for everyone if her momma could raise her in her birth country. But at the time, I was so overcome with grief and emotion and anger, that I could not think clearly. The rug had been pulled out from under us. Or as Kalyn has since pointed out to me, we no longer had a rug; we we struggling to stand on threads, and those had now been set on fire. We had nowhere left to go. We allowed ourselves to believe this time it was really happening because we had the official referral. I was naïve enough to think there was no way this could happen right after all the devastation we had faced the last few months. To be told we had a daughter...again...and then to be told "maybe not," shook us.

Kelsey called at almost three in the morning our time telling us that the baby girl's momma took her home. Vince did not sleep a wink, and I slept very little.

Instead, I found myself talking to God most of the night. At that point in my life, I questioned if He was even there. Not everyone believes in God or a higher power, but I always did.

I began believing when I was seven years old. When he was just a month old, my brother was in the hospital with a serious illness, and he wasn't expected to live. I prayed harder than ever and begged God to let him live. I felt something that no words can explain, and felt Him tell me everything would work out. The very next day, my brother's blood work came back perfect. Within a week, he was home.

The doctors had no explanation. He was the first infant in the United States to survive a Yersinia infection. He was in the medical books for years. From that moment on, I believed, even when friends did not, even when prayers went unanswered, even when I saw the evil in the world.

But this past year had tested my faith...I felt like every prayer I had from that year had been unanswered. I lost my grandpa, I lost Stormy, and now I felt like I had lost my daughter. I know that sounds fatalistic again, but at the time, I felt lost and abandoned.

I begged God to give me a sign that everything would work out. Vince and I felt as if maybe we had gotten the signs mixed up...maybe it was time to drop out of the program. Maybe this wasn't for us.

> "To make a long story short, we lost the referral that night. We were also informed that this has never happened before after [receiving the] referral. While we are thankful that she gets to stay in her birth country with her mom, we are also heartbroken. We thought of her as our daughter for four days. And now we are back to the waiting and praying."

I finally fell asleep from exhaustion at approximately four in the morning, and when I awoke at just after six to get ready for school, I had a calming peace.

I had dreamt about a beautiful baby girl. The feeling that our daughter was out there was stronger than ever. I thought maybe this was God or the universe giving me the sign I needed, but I was also extremely jaded. So I kept the dream to myself and guarded my heart. I refused to allow myself to feel any kind of hope, because I felt that once I allowed myself to feel any hope at all, I would be disappointed all over again.

That next night, Vince asked me, "Do you have anything left? Do you want to continue? I won't be mad at all if you say no. This year has been pure hell."

I didn't want to tell him about the dream. I didn't feel right sharing it with anyone. It felt too personal.

Instead, I said, "It has been worse than hell. But giving up isn't the answer. Let's just keep going. What is supposed to happen, will happen. And who knows, maybe this will all make sense one day."

We finished out that last week of school and told Kelsey we were staying in the program. She informed us that most of the babies due that summer were girls and asked if we would prefer to wait for the next baby girl available. We could not bring ourselves to return the baby items we bought when we thought we had a daughter, so we didn't.

We asked her to keep us informed of any baby born, but if there happened to be a boy and a girl born around the same time, our preference would be a girl. If we could, we wanted to hold out for the daughter we felt we had out there. I felt selfish saying that out loud, but it also felt right, like we were meant to say it.

Our agency asking us if we'd like to wait on a girl seemed like a sign, since requesting gender was not allowed in the Japan program. So as of the end of May, we were waiting again, praying our little one would be in our arms soon, but terrified to feel any kind of hope.

> "Since then, we have been doing some soul-searching. We have to be honest and admit that we are terrified about proceeding forward, but are determined to see this through and bring home our little one. She was not our Everly Sky, but we are hoping we will bring home our Everly soon! Yes, we could still bring home a son, and we would be ecstatic either way. So for now, the girl clothes and shoes are in a bag in the nursery hoping to be opened and put away soon.
>
> There are eight babies due before June 26th. All of them could be US babies or none of them could be. The US part of the program has slowed down since March, but we are praying our little one will be ours soon. But this time, we will be much more guarded with our hearts and with sharing pictures with all of you. We hope you understand.
>
> We have our good days and our bad days. Some days we really miss our boy and I struggle not to spend my whole day crying, and others I smile at his memory. Some days, we miss the little girl who we thought was ours, but then other days we get excited thinking she gets to be with her mom and our little one will come along soon, hopefully. That is the whole purpose for why we show

you all the wonderful parts and all the hard parts of the adoption journey...we can only hope we are inspiring some of you to take a leap of faith or to just hold on to whatever it is you are struggling with in your lives."

After sharing the photos and details of our referral, we had to go back to that blog post and delete the pictures and the details. It was like losing her all over again. It was so much harder than I expected because I was "deleting" her from our life. To this day, I wonder about that sweet girl and her beautiful mother. But instead of sadness, I now feel such peace and joy. It's a wonderful place to be.

Once, I had someone ask me, "Isn't it hard sharing all the bad news with everyone?"

It struck me as an odd question. Of course it's hard. But after unpacking that question further, I think the better answer is that yes, it is hard, but it is also therapeutic. For someone who bottles her emotions up and hates feeling pitied, putting it out there for everyone to read was difficult, but helpful for me. It was a way to process everything we were going through. Not only was it cathartic for me, but we felt it was important for people to hear the good and the bad.

So many women planning to adopt or already in the adoption process reached out to me with questions and advice. So many thanked me for being transparent. It is so important for anyone planning to adopt to know the good and the bad, and that the pain is worth it. With all the ups and downs, getting to the finish line can be a struggle, and hopeful adoptive parents need to hear that. They need to know they are not alone.

CHAPTER 7

Maybe You're Wrong

Summer was officially upon us as June began, and eight babies were due before June 28. I wish I could tell you that I was feeling more confident that one of those sweet little ones would be ours, but that would be a lie. Every day stretched on and on, unbearably slow. The house felt lonely, empty without Stormy, and Jackie, our older pup, walked around lost, wondering where he was, and honestly, my heart was wondering the same. The glass case surrounding my bottled-up emotions shattered the day Stormy left us, and I had been devoured by the silent monster inside me.

Depression is not a word to be thrown around lightly. At the time, I never wanted to admit that maybe I was suffering from depression. I was embarrassed and felt broken and unworthy. But at this point, I started to question if how low I was feeling was normal. I think it is important not only to our story, but also for others, to discuss depression and the stigma surrounding the word. Why is it okay to talk about physical medical conditions but still taboo to mention mental illness?

I sat down one day and talked to Vince about my mental condition. I whispered the words I had avoided saying for months...

"I think I need help. Everything is getting to be too much for me to handle and process on my own. I have honestly never felt like this before and it's starting to scare me."

Vince was incredibly supportive and offered to help any way he could. I made an appointment with my family physician and laid it all out on the table for him.

As you may be wondering, when hopeful adoptive families have a home study completed, they also have to have a physician fill out a medical report. Many countries do not allow families to adopt when there is a history of mental illness or if the adoptive parents are on certain medications. I did not want anything to derail the adoption. I knew I needed help, but also felt that maybe I could "fix" myself without the strongest medicine available.

I thought all my symptoms were from my anxiety, but my doctor offered another idea. He believed I was truly suffering from anxiety and depression, but that I could possibly have a thyroid issue making the depression and anxiety worse. He put me on low-dose medication that would help combat my anxiety without jeopardizing our adoption since it was not considered anxiety medication, and he also ran a thyroid panel.

Two days later, his nurse called informing me that I did indeed suffer from Hypothyroidism, which can also lead to higher levels of anxiety and depression. So along with the emotional turmoil I had been trying to deal with, my thyroid was fueling the fire and leading to the perfect storm. I began taking a thyroid medication, along with the previously prescribed medicine to help with my anxiety and possible depression.

Then I was hit with yet another crippling blow. One of my aunts, Ruth, had been sick off and on and had test after test ran to see what could be wrong. It turned out to be Lyme Disease from years prior. With everything else going on, I had not been keeping up to date on her condition the way I should have been. I regret this immensely now. Her liver had begun shutting down, therefore she had been put on the list awaiting a liver transplant. She finally received a transplant in the late spring, but at the end of May, the anti-rejection medication began damaging her heart, and it was not monitored correctly.

She was admitted back into the hospital and was then placed in the ICU while they tried to help stabilize her, and we thought it was working. My uncle informed us that she just kept saying she wanted to meet our little one. She talked about us nearly every day and could not wait to hear updates. She was fighting hard.

Then one day, I remember the phone ringing and my dad on the other line: "Ash, Ruth passed away this morning. Nobody, not even the doctors, were expecting it. They suspect her heart gave out."

Once again, I felt the weight of yet another lost family member that would never meet our cherry blossom.

I know it does not make sense, even to myself, but I felt so guilty that we had not brought home a baby before Aunt Ruth passed away. We had no control over that, but once again, the anxiety and depression took hold of me and I could not shake the guilt, like it was somehow my fault. The anxiety had to be beaten, but I was scared to face it.

Ashamed is the only word I can think of to describe my feelings toward the medication. It was as if my body and mind were working together with the universe to destroy me. There I go, being all fatalistic again... But it took a long time for me to admit to anyone, even my very best friends, that I was taking medication. That is not okay.

It is not okay that people who are already suffering from debilitating anxiety and depression, or any other mental demons, should feel ashamed to admit they are getting help for those issues. People suffering from mental illness are not defective or any less of a person, and when they are reaching out to get help, that should be celebrated, not kept secret.

So for those who are currently suffering, I want to encourage you to get help, reach out, find a support system. For those who are receiving help in one way or another, I applaud you for taking that all too important first step. Don't hide in the shadows...the more people who stand up and fight against the stigma of mental health, the easier it becomes for those behind us.

By the middle of June, the medication started to help, but I knew it was going to be a long, slow road. This type of medication does not help overnight, and my doctor had told me not to expect a quick recovery, and that we would need to adjust the medications as needed over time until we get the dosage correct.

We had heard from our agency twice about babies being born, but we kept our hearts guarded. Privately, I began researching Sheltie rescues to keep myself occupied so I was not obsessing over the adoption. In hindsight, this was not healthy either. I knew I needed to grieve my boy longer before adopting a new pup, but our home felt so empty. I missed that classic Sheltie bark and grieved that Sheltie butt wiggle on walks. I mourned the Sheltie herding mentality, and the way Stormy was always by my side, the best shadow. Vince said we were not ready, especially because we would be heading to Japan and welcoming home a newborn soon. He was definitely correct, but once again, fate intervened.

My mom, who Vince jokingly calls "an enabler," came across a photo of a sweet eight-week old Sheltie puppy who had a slight overbite and needed a home quickly before being taken to a shelter. She could not be a show dog because of her overbite, so she was deemed a family dog only. Perfect for us. Stormy and my first Sheltie from my childhood, Foxy, were both blue merle Sheltie boys. This sweet girl was a sable and white merle female, the complete opposite.

Meet Sadie

Against Vince's better judgement, we picked her up a few short days after seeing her photo. Vince was trying everything to be supportive. He

83

knew I was hanging by a thread and wanted to help bring a smile to my face. If that meant bringing home a new pup, then so be it. I also felt better that she was, in a way, a rescue. Because of one small imperfection, she had been deemed unworthy, but I wanted to show her she could be loved the way she deserved. This was something I could control or "fix," and that was what I needed at the time.

We named our new family member Sadie and prayed her sibling would be home soon so they could grow up together. Looking back, I know Sadie was a distraction from the chaos in our lives. That sounds terrible, I understand, but taking her on adventures and showering her with love kept the grief and anxiety at bay a little. She kept us from emailing our agency every single day for an update. And for that, I am forever indebted to our Sadie girl. And don't be fooled...Vince was wrapped around her tiny paw within a week. I have a tiny puppy Cleveland Cavaliers jersey he bought her to prove it.

The last week of June was upon us and all babies that had been born were either being adopted domestically in Japan, adopted by a waiting Canadian family, or were to be raised by their loving biological families. We were exhausted from the waiting. We were drained from the ups and downs.

Then came a late night email from Kelsey. I grabbed my phone and read the email immediately with hope-filled eyes...

"Hey, Ashley. There's a situation I'd like to ask you about..."

She went on to describe a special situation with a baby who had just been born. We discussed the baby's file and ultimately decided this sweet little one belonged to another waiting family because we felt unprepared for this unique situation.

Because this was so private and personal, I will not delve into further details, but just know that this sweet child is now with the perfect family and is happy and healthy, and for that, I can smile. At the time though, it felt like yet another blow to us. Another family behind us on the list was welcoming home their baby, and we were still waiting.

While the waiting was excruciating, I will say that it gave me a much needed lesson in the value of patience. I fully admit I'm a horribly impatient person. I'm not good at waiting for anything, whether it is the cake and ice cream I know I am having for a birthday celebration or a trip I am planning. The minute I know about something good headed my way, I obsess over it.

But as I have mentioned a few times already, I learned a valuable lesson in not wishing our lives away once we found out Stormy and my Papaw Bud were both sick. I learned that each day, every single minute, is a blessing.

I like to think Vince and I did well for the most part and enjoyed our time together as a couple, but as July rolled in and we were celebrating Independence Day, we were emotionally worn down. The way a runner is worn out by the end of the marathon, or the way I imagine a single parent might feel after working all day and staying up with a crying baby all night. Once again, we began to question whether this path was truly meant for us.

But I still could not shake the feeling that our baby was already in the world. I felt as if my grasp on reality must be slipping, because I knew that had to be impossible, or at least, very unlikely since our program was matching parents with infants less than six weeks old. Still...I held onto that feeling with everything in me.

A few days after July 4th, we received an email that another baby girl had been born and was planning on going to a family in the US. Kelsey said she would keep us updated as she began to receive paperwork and photos from Japan.

This time I refused to feel any excitement. This was now the eighth time we had been told about a baby and the eighteenth baby to be born since we became first on the waiting list. I locked away the tiny flicker of hope that sparked inside me and refused to allow it to become a full-grown flame.

As we had come to expect, two days later we received yet another email from our agency letting us down easy. Once again, this little girl was not meant to be ours. This time my heart didn't break quite as much. This time it felt okay, as if I somehow already knew this sweet baby was not our daughter.

I still felt our little one, and the feeling was stronger than ever. Maybe that was the reason I accepted the news better than previous times, or maybe I had grown to expect bad news. I'm not sure.

Vince and I once again kept busy with trips to the zoo and going on hikes with our pups. I had girls' day brunches with my favorite gals and kept a smile plastered on my face while informing them of the latest updates. I did express my fears and concerns as well, but always said I was holding it together.

Those days were also very therapeutic because they made me feel somewhat normal and human. I can't stress enough the importance of having a support system. Whether you are sharing good news, tragic news, or just living life, it is so crucial to have friends and family by your side. Without the support of some of the very best friends a gal could ask for and the love of our families, I'm pretty confident we would have given up before reaching the finish line. When the finish line is constantly moving, you never know when the marathon will end, when you will get to catch your breath. But you keep pushing yourself because your supporters are there cheering you on and rooting for you. They are the ones giving you that extra drive and encouragement to keep moving, even if you are only crawling sometimes.

Then came the day that almost broke me, the day I almost told Vince I was done. I received a message from Tomomi. As I recall the words she sent me that day, I can now realize how careful she was being with me:

"Hey, so I really want you to hear this from me. We heard from Kelsey, and there is a little one whose first mom chose us."

The message went on from there.

She felt she needed to reach out and let me know she had been contacted by our agency and there was an expectant mother who wanted them to be her sweet daughter's family. As previously mentioned, in the Japan program, birth moms have a say in which families they wish to place their babies into. Tomomi and I had become so close, and she was always there inspiring us along this journey. She wanted me to be the first to know, outside of their family, that they might be bringing a daughter home. Boy, did this sting pretty badly.

I felt the panic clawing its way up my throat. My lungs were constricted and the tears stung my eyes terribly. I was torn in two.

I told her I was so thrilled for her, and that was not a lie. She is an incredible woman, with an amazing family. But this hurt. I felt, once again, that we were being told by the universe we were not good enough. We were just not enough, and maybe we never would be.

Tomomi understood. She knew exactly how I felt. She said she understood if I was upset, angry, frustrated, and everything else in between. If I needed to distance myself from her, she would leave me alone for a while.

All of this made me hurt fiercely, but it also made me love her even more. Of course I did not want to distance myself from her. I wanted to celebrate with her if and when she brought home her daughter. I did not care how badly it broke me, I would not distance myself from the woman who had been through so much with me, who helped me get through the hardest year of my life. I told Tomomi she had better not distance herself and that she must keep me informed every step of the way.

After talking with Tomomi that day, I took Sadie outside and just sat in Stormy's favorite part of our backyard. I let the tears fall, leaving tracks down my cheeks. After sitting and trying to just feel and not think about the adoption, the tears slowed, my breathing became more even, and I felt more at peace. The breeze on that unseasonably cool July day somehow refreshed me and I felt more hopeful. I played with Sadie for a little while and then walked inside, ready to tackle the next part of our journey, whatever that would be.

A Small Update[9]

"So we cannot and do not wish to say a lot here. In the adoption world, there is a lot of privacy and different things we are allowed to say and not say and we sometimes have to figure out what is appropriate and what should probably not be put out there.

We have been informed by our agency that there have been a couple babies born over the last several days and there are several upcoming due dates as well... One of these babies should be released to the Japanese agency's custody early next week...we do not know yet if this sweet baby will qualify for the USA...it will depend on the family situation. At this time we are praying and hoping that no matter what happens, the birth family feels peace and comfort with whatever decision is made. At the same time it is hard not to hope and pray this little one is ours, but we feel the most important thing is that it works out in the best interest of the family and the baby.

One thing we love about this program is that birth moms get to have a say in where their babies get placed. Some request that there be a certain religion in the household, a certain number of children, or even for a family to have Japanese heritage if at all possible. Some babies have skipped over us because of certain circumstances beyond our control, but that's okay. It does sting, but at the same time, we are just happy that the birth family is comfortable and at peace with their decision and that these precious little ones are with the best possible families for them. Our time will come...

We have been so close for so long, but we feel it is working out

---

[9] *Our blog post on our website posted on July 21, 2017.*

exactly how it is supposed to; we may not understand why it is unfolding the way it is at this time, but we just hope our time is getting closer. We are both mentally and emotionally exhausted...it has been a long and emotional five months now."

The same day as we posted this blog, we were told about another little one. The feeling our child was out there was getting stronger, but a small part of me felt as if this sweet girl would, once again, not be our daughter.

As we were awaiting news, Vince asked me, "How are you feeling about this little one? Are you hopeful?" A little piece of my heart still hoped she was our daughter, but I responded honestly...

"No. I don't think she is our daughter. I am hopeful that I am wrong, but I don't think I am. But," I continued, "Vince, our daughter is out there. I know you don't understand, but I feel her. I can't explain it, but she will be in our arms soon."

CHAPTER 8

JUST KEEP GOING

The day after hearing from Tomomi, Kelsey emailed us about another baby, also a girl, who was most likely going to be a US referral. Her momma had already even expressed wanting to meet us. This tiny piece of information actually inspired us to be a little more hopeful about this sweet girl. I still couldn't shake the feeling that our little one had been out in this world for months already, but I kept brushing that feeling aside. At this point, I just needed to hold on to hope that we would bring a baby home soon.

Vince was handling this about the same as I was; he was getting excited but was careful with those feelings as well.

He knew nights were the most difficult for me. Lying in bed, I would think about the what-ifs:

What if Stormy were still here with us? What if this baby is ours? What if we never get a referral? What if the program unexpectedly shuts down before we bring home a baby?

So we developed a nightly routine before falling asleep, staying up late discussing bedtime rituals and traditions we wanted to start with our future child, such as Friday pizza and movie nights, Christmas Eve bedtime stories in matching pajamas, mommy-and-me shopping trips, and father-daughter date nights. It was nice dreaming about our future instead of focusing on our past and how the last year had unfolded. That kept us going.

I had also begun to question our decision to hold out for a daughter. After losing our referral, we had told Kelsey we wanted to try to hold out for a girl. We felt it was a sign. But Vince and I had discussed that if we did not become parents by August 1, maybe we should reevaluate that decision. That date was quickly creeping up on us. By this point in July, there had only been one boy born that we knew of that passed us on the list.

Vince and I desperately wanted to be parents, and we were constantly on the lookout for "signs" as to what decision to make at any given time. Yes, we were still scared, like all future parents are, but the excitement outweighed that fear for the first time in a long time. I desperately hoped that meant our time was finally nearing.

One night, while watching old episodes of *Friends*, Vince looked over at me and said, "It's going to happen soon. I can feel it. For the first time in months, I really feel hopeful and excited. Something feels different."

"I feel it too," I admitted. "And I think we should keep her name Everly Sky."

Vince agreed. We had been considering changing the name we had chosen since we had named the sweet girl from our first referral Everly, but I felt that name was the name of our daughter, whoever she was and wherever she may be.

On July 26, Kelsey emailed:

"Hi, Ashley...I received news from [the agency in Japan] this morning that the birth mother of the baby girl has decided to parent. She informed them on the day in which they were supposed to receive custody."

We were happy...we really were. Yes, we were feeling yet another blow to our confidence, but it was nice to hear of another little one having the opportunity to remain in her birth country with her family.

Kelsey went on to say, "I know the wait feels unbearable at times, especially when you see other families passing you by. I'm continuing to pray that we see the sweet baby that is meant to be yours soon."

Vince and I were so thankful for Kelsey and her words. She always helped us feel stronger and supported on this journey. We talked and decided to let Kelsey know that very same day that we could not handle receiving anymore updates. We asked her back in the spring to keep us updated on all births, but it had become too daunting for us. It was heartbreaking and exhausting. The constant ups and downs had caused my anxiety to worsen, even with the medication I was taking.

So we asked her to only contact us once a referral was waiting for us and she understood completely. She wrote us a sweet email that said, "I know right now you don't understand, but I promise one day this will all make sense. I have seen it happen before. Your story is one for the books. Everything you have been through is leading you to the little one meant to be in your family. Just keep going. I promise one day you'll understand, and I will be right there celebrating with you."

I read those words over and over, and I prayed she was right. I'm not sure if she truly understood at the time or even now today, but Kelsey is one reason Vince and I held on and made it to the end of this journey. I will never be able to repay the strength she gave us. I am immensely grateful the universe brought her into our lives.

Kelsey concluded the email by saying she would be in touch once she had a referral ready to go or if she had a special circumstance pop up that she needed to discuss with us. She warned us it would most likely be a few weeks or even months, unless a special situation arose. We thanked her profusely for everything and said we hoped to hear from her sooner rather than later.

That night, I sat down and started a letter to our "future little one." I could not find all the right words, so I went to bed and decided to try again the next morning. I had the best night of sleep I had experienced in a very long time. I woke up feeling refreshed, recharged, and re-energized for the remaining wait.

Vince noticed and asked, "Well, why are you in such a chipper mood this morning?"

I thought about it for a second and really couldn't come up with an answer. I just smiled, shrugged my shoulders, and walked into the living room to finish my letter to our future child. I finished it around noon and put it in the adoption journal I had been keeping. When I sat down and began writing this memoir, I knew that letter was the perfect way to start. The letter you read at the very beginning of this book is the letter I finished writing on the morning of Thursday, July 27, 2017. Remember this date.

Vince and I took the pups for a walk that afternoon down at the park and had a normal, fun day, free from stress, which felt wonderful. I have no idea what changed overnight, but I felt incredibly joyful. At the time, I attributed it to the glorious nine hours of deep, restful sleep and to Kelsey's words in the email the previous day, but it was a strange feeling after months of worry, sadness, and anxiety.

Sadie's first trip to the Reservoir for a walk

We were preparing for the gruesome wait without the constant updates we had come to expect. But little did we know our lives were about to change that night. God really does know what He is doing, and this time it was so much better than anything we expected or felt we truly deserved.

CHAPTER 9

HAVING FAITH

Faith and Fate[10]

"I'm going to tell you a story, a story that seems almost unbelievable. It's a story of hope as well as hopelessness, with a major dose of faith and fate. It's an ending to a much larger story really, but at the same time, the beginning of an even larger, more amazing story that is yet to unfold...

On Monday, July 24, we were informed by our agency that yet another baby we hoped could have been ours was not meant to be. The baby's birth mom chose to raise her. Since April, we have been close so many times, but something seemed to keep standing in our way. But even though our faith was wavering, we knew those babies ended up with their families, the families they were meant to be a part of.

After hearing once again that this baby was not going to be our little one, we told our agency to only update us once the Japanese agency had custody of a baby or if a special situation would suddenly arise. We just could not keep getting our hopes up only to be told that once again our little one had not yet been born. All our agency could tell us was that there must be a specific child out there meant to be ours. We tried really hard to believe this, and I

---

[10] *Our blog post on our website posted on August 11, 2017.*

think a big part of us did believe it. But grief and despair and impatience are strong beasts, and they completely overshadowed that faith we had deep down.

I'm going to be transparent, the next few days following this news were hard. I was in a pretty low place. But I started trying to get my mind focused on other things...I even decided to write our future cherry blossom a letter. I thought that would be therapeutic in a way. I wrote this letter on Thursday morning, July 27, and it gave me some peace. I was in a much better place."

Thursday, July 27 felt different. I thought maybe it was the medication finally kicking in, or maybe my body was tired of feeling hopeless and defeated. As I sit here writing this over two years later, my mind has another option: maybe my heart and soul knew that day would be the day our lives would change forever in the best way. I don't know, and of course we never will know why I felt so alive that day for the first time in a very long time, but it doesn't matter. The email we received right before falling asleep is what matters.

At exactly 12:22 am, Vince and I were lying in bed. I was reading on my phone and he was just plugging his phone in and setting his alarm. Right as he rolled over and I was closing my Kindle app, I saw a notification from my email account pop across my screen. It was Kelsey.

My heart skipped a beat and I felt dizzy. I could not take in enough air. There was no way she would email this late or at all unless she had something important to explain or ask us.

I smacked Vince in the back. He responded with, "Ow, what the heck?"

I shushed him and told him we just received an email from Kelsey. He sat straight up and said, "Well, don't just sit there. Open it."

I took a deep breath and opened the email at 12:25 am, July 28, 2017. The words I read will forever be etched on my heart. I won't leave the entire email here, as it included some personal information, but in short, the email stated that she could not wait until morning to reach out to us. Kelsey had just received an email from the agency in Japan about a baby that was born May 11, 2017, who possibly needed a home very soon.

The Japanese agency would be meeting with this momma in just a few days and would potentially take custody of this little one at that time if that was the decision this brave momma made. Kelsey just needed to know if we were okay with proceeding on this adoption of a sweet girl who was a tad older than the traditional newborn and who will probably be attached to her first momma more so than a newborn.

I knew what my heart was screaming, but this was our decision, not just mine. I asked him his thoughts. I looked at Vince and he looked at me.

"The fact that she will be three months old does not bother me at all," he responded. "In the grand scheme of life, so what?"

I smiled and said, "I'm happy you said that. I think this is it. I can feel it. Maybe this is the reason."

Vince asked me what I meant by "the reason," and I explained that maybe this was our why. We had been searching and praying and asking the universe why the delays. Why were we the first couple in the ten plus year history of the Japan program to have so many things go "wrong"? Why were we not meant to parent any of those sweet babies?

This was our answer — because we were meant to parent this beautiful girl. She was meant to be our daughter.

Another sign I mentioned to Vince was her date of birth. As unstoppable tears fell from my eyes, I explained to him that the day in May that Stormy felt better before passing away was May 11. I had chills remembering that beautiful day. It was as if he was trying to tell me it would all be okay, because he was sending me a daughter to help us through. This also explained that feeling I carried with me all through most of May, June, and July that our baby was out there already. I finally truly understood that feeling. The peace that settled over me was so tangible. This finally felt right.

So we sent a reply to Kelsey just before 12:45 am exclaiming, "Yes, yes, we would love to proceed!" Vince and I sat up staring at the ceiling for at least an hour. I fell asleep around 3:30 am and dreamed of Japan.

The first thing I did upon awakening was check my phone, and there was an email waiting for me. It read, "I had a feeling I knew the answer, but wanted to reach out anyway."

She went on to say how strange it is sometimes how things work out. Just two days ago, I told her we did not want anymore updates until a referral was ready or unless a special situation presented itself. We thought we would be waiting at least a few weeks to hear from her. Then just days later, this happened.

She informed us that she told our agency in Japan we were interested and to show this beautiful mom our photos and file. They were set to meet with her on August 2, so we would not hear more until after the meeting with her. Those next five days would feel ridiculously long.

> "The agency in Tokyo met with the mother and counseled her on August 2. She decided to continue with her original plan and to go the US route. They showed her our file and she signed off on us!"

On the morning of August 2, Kelsey emailed informing us that the Japanese agency had just taken custody of this sweet girl. Referral would not take as long as usual because most of the paperwork was already completed since she was a little older.

Let me explain here. Part of the paperwork that takes the longest in Japan is the family registry. That is similar to a birth certificate here in the US, but in Japan, the government issues the family registry where they record the entire family history, and therefore it takes two to four weeks for it to be completed and sent to the agency in Tokyo. This almost three-month-old baby girl had her registry completed already. The rest of the paperwork would take less than two weeks to complete, so Kelsey said we could receive the referral anytime between August 10-15. That was quick, and we were beginning to panic.

As teachers, the beginning of the school year is hectic. We were set to start workdays on Monday, August 14, and the first day with students was set for August 16. The last thing Vince and I wanted to do was jinx ourselves, but we knew we had to talk to our principal. We went in and discussed with him what we knew, but that everything was subject to change. He was incredibly understanding and supportive and began looking for long-term substitutes for both of us, which was a huge weight off our shoulders.

Vince and I were over the moon, but because of our past history, we tried to keep our hearts guarded. We also felt a deep sadness for this little girl who was grieving her momma and for this beautiful mother who had most likely just made the most difficult decision of her life, and was grieving for her little girl. We threw ourselves into work and began completing lesson plans for the first two weeks of school just in case, re-packing for Japan, and buying larger baby items for a three-month-old baby girl. While doing all of this, we had to remain open to the idea that this may fall through and all this planning and organizing would be for nothing.

On August 5, Kelsey informed us that things were moving right along and we told her we could travel any time. She decided to go ahead and request an appointment with the US Embassy to see when we could be interviewed. She said not to expect a date before August 21, but there was a small chance they could have an earlier appointment. With great shock, the Embassy granted us an appointment for Tuesday, August 15, which meant we could be booking flights for August 11 or 12. We could not believe it. Everything was falling into place so perfectly and so quickly. I just kept waiting on something to go wrong, but every email had more news propelling us forward to the day we would be heading to Japan.

We had learned our lesson from the lost referral in May, so as of August 6, we had still only told our closest friends, our immediate families, and our boss about this potential referral. We also spoke with Adoption Airfare and had them hold plane tickets for us for Saturday morning, August 12.

Kelsey was emailing us every day with new info, new forms, and even a couple of photos. The first photo we saw was sent to us

One of the first photos we have of Everly

around 6:00 pm while we were on our way out to my parents' house on August 7. I was driving and I remember being so anxious to get to their house so I could see her. But as I'm sure you can understand after reading our journey so far, a small part of me was terrified to look. What if her first mom came back for her? I could not fall in love with a photo again, just to lose her. But I did look, and my heart instantly fell for this chubby-cheeked, crazy-haired, beautiful baby girl. My heart knew in that instant she was our daughter. She was the one I knew even back in high school that I would one day be blessed to parent. She was the answer to every prayer I had sent in the last few years. She is what made this journey make complete sense.

We went in and showed my parents and brother and then went to show Vince's mom. We sent the photo to his brother Nick, our sister-in-law and my best friend Erica, and Vince's sister Haley. I also sent the photo to my other two best gals, Kalyn and Michael.

I messaged Tomomi of course, and she was thrilled for us. She was actually in Japan at that very moment meeting her daughter. I felt such overwhelming joy for her. We had come full circle; we were both bringing home daughters at the same time.

On August 9, 2017, we received the official referral at 4:00 pm. We read through the social report and cried. Her first momma had an amazing story and we could tell from this twelve-page report that she loved her daughter fiercely.

> "Her given name is Mizuki, which comes from the Japanese word for the flowering dogwood tree. It means 'beautiful moon.' How perfect and incredibly beautiful is that? So her name once she comes home will be Everly Sky Mizuki Banion."

As I'm sure you are beginning to understand, we will not share more details of her story. This is for us and our sweet daughter and her first momma to know. But understand that every single word was ingrained into our heads and our hearts. We will one day share the story with our Everly, leaving nothing out because it is her story and her past. We looked through twenty photos of our daughter, two of which we cherish a little more than the others since they show her with her first mom. I am so incredibly thankful to have those for Everly one day. Anyone who saw those photos could see the love this beautiful, brave momma felt — and will always feel — for the daughter we would now share.

On the evening of August 11, the day our daughter turned three months old on the other side of the world, I wrote a blog post introducing her. We finally felt comfortable sharing. We packed up the last of our items, including presents for the staff at the Japanese agency and a gift for Everly's first momma that I hope she received along with the letter we wrote for her.

We slept maybe an hour because our nerves were all over the place and my anxiety held me hostage as I thought about what the next few days would look like thousands of miles from home. Those fears Vince and I had over becoming parents crept back up into my head that night. I was beginning to doubt it all and wonder how in the world we would pull this off, especially being in a hotel room in a foreign country.

While frantically triple checking that we had everything packed and our lesson plans complete that morning, I sat down and cried.

"Hey, what's wrong?" Vince asked me.

"I don't even know," I responded while simultaneously laughing and crying. "I am just so completely overwhelmed. I feel like I am turning in circles, and I know we have forgotten to do or to pack something."

Vince understood and in his usual way, played the calm one. "I get it. But guess what? As long as we have the paperwork needed to bring her home, we will be just fine because in my eyes, that is all we need."

"I guess. I just want everything to be perfect. I want us to be perfect...for her. What if we aren't? What if we have no idea what to do once we have her in our arms?"

"Well, go ahead and throw those thoughts out the window, honey. Nothing is ever going to go completely as planned. And we are nowhere near perfect; nobody is. It's going to be okay though. We are about to meet our daughter for the very first time, and we are going to learn as we go, just like every single parent in the history of the world does. Just focus on the minute we get to meet Everly."

I knew he was right. I took a deep breath and helped him load the luggage into the car.

> "It still seems so surreal! We will be boarding a plane Saturday morning and will be returning home next Friday afternoon with a beautiful baby girl. We will officially be parents. *Cue the freak out!"

Vince tried reassuring me multiple times, and sometimes I believed him and other times I felt as if I would vomit. He had the same fears I had, but was so good at being positive and remaining calm. I was a bundle of nerves, but he helped me feel some sort of peace before arriving at the airport.

On the morning of August 12, we boarded a plane, with my mom tagging along to help us become parents for the first time, and set forth on a twelve-hour plane ride to meet our girl.

"Even when we had to search deep inside ourselves for the faith to carry on and believe our little one would find us, it was there. We still had faith that what was meant to be would be. Fate is an interesting little character, and she worked her magic on our journey. God knew what He was doing from the start, and even when we thought this day would never come, He knew it would. So this may be the conclusion of the waiting, of this part of the story, but it is just the beginning to a much larger and more amazing story...the story of the rest of our lives..."

PART III

Japan

CHAPTER 10

SHE'S HERE, AND SHE'S PERFECT

Japan. What an amazingly beautiful country. As I mentioned before, I fell in love with the country from the first moment I stepped on Japanese soil in 2012.

Well, that may be an exaggeration...remember, the first moment we stepped on Japanese soil in 2012, our luggage was still in Chicago, lost somewhere at the airport, and we were literally stuck in the bus station and could not figure out how to scan our ticket to physically exit the building. There were tears...lots and lots of tears.

But on day two, I truly fell in love with Japan and the people who give the country life.

This time, though, Japan held an even deeper and more meaningful place in my heart. When I stepped off the plane on Sunday, August 13, this time with our luggage, I knew I was in my daughter's home country. We were on the same continent for the first time. The emotions flooded me. I was almost paralyzed by the fear, excitement, anxiety, happiness, and sadness. I still don't understand how I functioned. I was just putting one foot in front of the other and running on autopilot.

As any new parent feels, Vince and I were scared and anxious about becoming parents, especially in a hotel room on the other side of the world. We were also more excited than we had ever been and felt such joy.

Speaking of the hotel room, I feel compelled to explain that my mom and I learned our lesson from 2012. Hotel rooms in Japan are notoriously tiny. Picture an average hotel room here in America and then cut it nearly in half and then you have the average hotel room size in Japan. Some even have traditional rooms where there is a cot or mat on the floor. We did our research and booked an "American style" hotel as it was advertised. It was still slightly smaller than an American hotel room, and had three twin beds instead of larger beds, but we made it work.

Even though we were filled with joy, we were also feeling a sadness deep within. With any adoption, there comes grief. Somewhere in Japan, a mother was grieving for the child she tried so hard to raise and a sweet three-month-old baby girl wondered where her momma was at night when she was falling asleep. The magnitude of that loss struck me hard. The pain I felt for our daughter and her first mom gutted me. It felt hard to catch my breath at times when I would think about the pain and loss they were both experiencing.

I think as adoptive parents, it is important to address that loss. Do I think adoption should be celebrated? Yes. Is adoption beautiful? Yes. But adoption starts with a tremendous loss, and it is impossible to fully comprehend that before the moment your little one is placed into your arms. Your heart breaks when she cries and grieves for everything she has lost. You smile when she smiles at you, while hoping that means she is beginning to accept you. You feel such gratitude and complete and utter love when you hold her at night while she's fast asleep peacefully in your arms because she feels safe, and you are so incredibly thankful to be holding her — finally — after months or even years of waiting. But you also grieve with her because you know what has been ripped away from her, and the importance of those feelings is not lost on you.

The day we arrived in Japan, I was a bundle of nerves. I barely remember the trip to the hotel from the airport. I remember being on a shuttle staring out the window, wringing my hands from the anxiety and trying my hardest not to vomit. I don't think Vince, Mom, and I said two words. We were each deep in our own thoughts, along with being emotionally and physically exhausted from a twelve-hour flight.

The one memory that does stand out from the shuttle to the hotel was when the beautiful social worker from the agency in Japan messaged me a photo of her three adorable kids welcoming us to their country and saying congrats on our baby girl. It was the sweetest gesture and brought tears to my eyes. That one message calmed me a little as we continued making our way into the heart of Tokyo.

"Hello!" the front desk attendant said cheerfully as we walked up to the counter.

Vince gave him our names and confirmed that we would be staying for five nights. "Also," Vince added, "we are in Japan adopting a three-month old baby girl. Tomorrow morning, the social worker will be bringing her to us. They told us to let you know to be expecting them."

The hotel staff was incredibly friendly as we explained the reason for being in Tokyo and that a little one would be joining us the next morning. I think they were a little taken aback by the fact we were adopting from Japan, but they were extremely helpful and supportive. International and domestic adoption were both extremely uncommon in Japan, and the front desk attendant at the time said he had never heard of such a thing, but thought it was an "incredible gesture." At the time, the Embassy had been processing between 30-40 international adoptions a year, with only 12-15 a year to the US.

After finishing check-in procedures and discussing international adoption a bit, the nice man smiled at us and said, "Well, we are happy to have you at our hotel. We hope your stay is wonderful and we are thankful for you adopting one of our orphaned children."

The sentiment was sweet as he "thanked" us, so we smiled and thanked him back. Inside, I cringed slightly at the words he used, but I truly felt he was happy for us and thankful, and trying to put those feelings into English the best that he could. It just felt strange to me that we were being thanked for adopting a baby that we had been longing and praying for.

By the time we made it up to our room and dropped our luggage on the carpeted floor, it was a little after seven in the evening. We decided to go to the hotel restaurant and eat a late dinner. My mom and I indulged in the delicious and filling Italian pasta (yes, we ate Italian food while in Japan...don't judge us), and Vince finished off a plate of traditional Japanese food. We were stuffed as we walked back to our room to relax and prepare for the morning.

To keep myself busy and my brain preoccupied, I bagged up all the gifts we brought for the staff at our Japanese agency and for Everly's first momma. Traditionally in Japan, people give gifts as a sign of respect and as a gesture of thankfulness. We were informed that we should bring gifts for the staff and nannies. We ended up buying way too much, as I am always guilty of.

We purchased locally grown tea bags, buckeye candy to represent Ohio, and other delicious American snacks for the two men who were on staff. We added in bath bombs for the wonderful female social worker from the agency (the one who had messaged me when we landed). One of my best friends, Kalyn, had aprons made for the nannies on staff to go along with the saltwater taffy we bought. And last, but certainly not least, we bought a special gift for our daughter's first momma to always remind her of the daughter we share.

We all showered and crashed before ten that night. As I lay in bed, staring up into the darkness, my mind raced, my stomach churned from the frantic butterflies, and my head spun, causing me to feel lightheaded. Once again, the fears and doubts crept back into my head...or perhaps they never really left.

I felt weak and doubted my ability and my worth. Was I enough for this little girl who was about to lose her first family and her culture?

Right then, I made a vow and whispered it into the universe. I vowed to give her every ounce of love I possessed. I vowed to do my very best, which is all any of us can do. And I vowed to give her as much of her

Japanese culture as we could. We are already planning our first trip to Japan together for when she is five, right before she enters kindergarten. It will be her first time back since leaving at just three months old, and it won't be our last trip back together, either. We are also going to be introducing the Japanese language and learning it together. We eat Japanese food once a week (or more) and we will tell her everything we can about her first family and the country she once called home.

Morning came, and none of us could sleep any longer. The sun was barely above the horizon, but we were wide awake. At eight in the morning, we decided to walk to the nearest Starbucks and get breakfast. The familiarity of the restaurant calmed my nerves some as I sat eating some sort of a green donut and drinking a warm drink that I could not name. I couldn't taste anything. Nothing was registering.

We sat in silence, all three of us, barely eating, barely breathing. We were all snapped out of our thoughts when my phone buzzed. It was the social worker saying good morning and informing us that instead of noon, they would be at our hotel an hour earlier. I glanced at the time on my phone and realized Everly would be in our arms in less than two hours. We threw away the rest of what we could not eat and promptly headed back to the hotel.

The hour and a half we waited in the room was almost unbearable. It was as if time had completely stopped. Then we heard it, the soft knock, and we all sat there on the bed staring at the closed door, as if willing it to pop open on its own.

My mom broke the silence. "Well, don't just sit there...go open the door."

I hopped off the bed and willed my stiff legs to move forward. Vince was right behind me as timid and frightened as I was. Looking back now, I can laugh. What a sight it must have been...two adults standing at our closed door terrified of a tiny baby on the other side of it.

I took a deep breath and looked at Vince. He nodded and I opened the door.

There she was.

I barely acknowledged the social worker or the nanny that had accompanied her. I could not take my eyes off the chunky girl with wild, unruly hair. My heart almost stopped and it was as if I was under water. Everything sounded distant, muffled. Every single part of my being was focused on our daughter.

Vince kindly moved me aside and motioned for them to come in. I followed them into the room and finally smiled at both women welcoming them. The nanny said in almost perfect English, "Would you like to hold her?"

My eyes snapped to hers and I blushed in embarrassment. "Oh, of course!"

She placed her in my arms and tears sprung to my eyes for the hundredth time since arriving the day before in Japan. She was finally here. We were together. Vince stood beside me, both of us staring down at her saying, "Hi!" in that singsong voice all parents develop. She looked right at us and smiled. And in that moment, I felt the anxiety seep from me. It felt so freeing.

Yes, I was still afraid. The new parent fears were still present, but I also felt such love, that it was almost unbearable. My heart felt whole and broken at the same time. I knew nothing else mattered except keeping her safe and loving her however she needed throughout her life.

We walked her over to my mom. Everly is her first, and maybe only, grandchild. She was over the moon in love immediately.

Gigi holds Everly for the first time.

Everly seemed to warm up to all of us right away — I couldn't believe it. It seemed too good to be true.

109

We talked to the nanny and the social worker about her napping and feeding schedule, how she behaved, her habits and personality, and everything else they felt we needed to know. They even handed us a booklet logging every time she ate, cried, and even pooped over the last twelve days that she was in their custody. We were very thankful, and to be honest, a little taken aback by the thoroughness and accuracy of the details.

Before they left, approximately thirty minutes after arriving, we handed them the gifts we had brought and scheduled a time to meet on Wednesday at the agency in order to sign the final paperwork. Then we said our goodbyes, and they were gone. It was just us and our daughter.

I remember looking at Mom and Vince saying, "Well, now what?"

They just laughed, and I joined in, but I was not joking. I had no clue what our next step should be. I can laugh now at how clueless we really were, but at the time, it was so overwhelming. The emotions are so hard to describe, but it was similar to getting married, graduating college, or the first day at a new job...you know it's wonderful and you are excited and ambitious and even in love with what is happening, but also afraid of making mistakes and terrified you are not strong enough or good enough for this next chapter you are about to embark on.

But of course we were going to make mistakes — we are only human after all. I knew that then, and I know that now, but I'll let you in on a little secret...I am still afraid of not being enough for Everly and of making mistakes. She deserves the best. I'm sure every parent has felt this way at least once. In the end, I realized that I just needed to take a deep breath and do the best I could for her. That's really all I could do, and I had to have faith that it would be enough.

So there we were. Just two new parents and one new grandma with this chubby, dark-eyed little girl staring up at us as if she already knew we were clueless. I remember laughing at the time about the look she was giving us. I'm sure she was thinking, "So this is what I'm stuck with, huh?"

I remember thinking to myself, "Yes, baby girl, you are stuck with us, and we are blessed with you."

We posted a few pictures on our social media accounts shortly after she arrived to keep our friends and family updated. We had no idea how to express what we were feeling at the time, so I kept it short and sweet:

"She's here, and she's perfect!"

Our first family photo

CHAPTER 11

NOT LEAVING

Day one with our daughter was fairly uneventful. Everly ate well, smiled constantly, and slept perfectly during her naps and the entirety of the first night with us in the hotel room. The only time she cried on that first day was when she was hungry.

We stayed in the room most of the day, only venturing out in the rain to go grab food for dinner. That night, Everly crashed around ten, so we all three fell into our beds as well.

I remember there was a thunderstorm that hit around the time she fell asleep in Vince's arms. Tears burned my eyes as I thought of Stormy. As I have mentioned, he hated thunder and would bark and run around the inside of the house during storms. After his passing in May, every storm reminded me of him and caused my breath to hitch and my heart to skip a beat. I remembered my dear friend Tomomi's words that Stormy was barking from the sky, letting me know he was there meeting his sister.

Everly awoke only one time during the night for a bottle at around three in the morning and then fell blissfully back asleep in my arms again. I held her for a few minutes just staring at her. It was hard to believe I was really in Japan holding the daughter I had longed for since I was sixteen years old. Some days, even now, I find it hard to believe and impossible to describe as my throat burns with emotion.

Vince and I woke up around eight and thought the most naive thoughts ever, giving ourselves pats on the back and congratulating ourselves for being A+ parents because day one went so smoothly. I'm confident God was chuckling about that time, easing us in with a false pretense of how "easy" this whole parenting gig was going to be. Because the next two days were ones for the record books ...

Everly laughing and playing in the hotel room on day two.

Day two, Tuesday, August 14, 2017, started off splendidly, then turned into a three-ring circus. We decided to eat in the hotel room and enjoy the overly exorbitant price of the same food we could have eaten downstairs, but spent twice as much on since they brought it to us. My mom pretended to read the Japanese newspaper and we giggled at Everly as she smiled and cooed.

We got dressed and ready to go fairly quickly so we would not be late. We were scheduled to meet with our guide that the agency provided for us. He was supposed to meet us at the medical center and then later again at the US Embassy. We had an appointment that morning to get Everly a wellness check and her Visa paperwork so we could then go to the US Embassy to present all paperwork and sign more papers later that afternoon.

After deciding on a taxi versus trying to navigate and tackle the public transportation in Tokyo, we hopped into a cab in front of our hotel. I am fairly confident the driver believed we had stolen our daughter. He kept looking back at us in the mirror, murmuring something we could not comprehend. At the time, I was scared he might take us to the local police station, but he surprised me by smiling and saying, "Have a good day," in broken English after pulling up in front of the medical building. By the way, we never would have found this building if we did not have a driver.

There was no sign or name at all on the building; it was a plain white building with a couple numbers in black on the side. We assumed we were in the right spot because we "recognized" our guide as he was the only one waving at us enthusiastically.

He walked over and in the reserved Japanese manner and introduced himself with a slight bow of respect. We followed him into the building to the second floor and he explained that we would meet with the doctor. She would weigh and measure Everly and address any concerns we might have. Then we would wait for the paperwork and be on our way. Sounded easy enough. Together we walked into a waiting room that looked like any normal waiting room you might find in America and sat down in uncomfortable plastic chairs by the door.

Up until that moment, Everly was a little pro. She sat quietly in her carrier strapped to my chest and smiled at everyone. But then we sat down. She apparently did not like that. She squirmed and fussed and forced me to get up to walk with her. That should have been a red flag that this may not be a pleasant experience.

After walking laps around the waiting room, we heard, "Vince and Ashley, please follow me."

Vince and I walked back to the cramped room and waited for the doctor. We were a little taken aback when in walked a white woman speaking with a British accent in the middle of Tokyo.

I instantly felt comfortable with her, and I'm sure it helped me knowing we could ask her questions and she would be able to clearly communicate with us. The feeling of isolation is powerful when in another part of the world where the culture, rules, and even language are not your own. After experiencing Japan twice, I can say that the anxiety I felt at being one of the only fluent English speakers in a crowd was perspective-altering. I have a whole new respect now for those in America who face that feeling every single day of their lives.

After introducing herself and asking about us and Everly, she weighed and

114

measured our girl.

"My, isn't she a little chunk!" she said. "She is a big girl."

She also commented on Everly's wild hair and "spunky" personality. See, we were beginning to already recognize the faces Everly made — and still makes now — when she is not amused. It was the look she gave us on day one, the look she gave us in the waiting room that day, and the look she was currently giving the doctor. Just imagine a typical teenage girl rolling her eyes at the mother who just told her to change her skirt because the length is not appropriate. Yeah...now you get it.

Anyway, Vince and I were curious about some darker spots on her skin, which turned out to be Mongolian Blue Spots and questioned the doctor about them, along with a subtle V that is a little pronounced on her forehead when she gets hot or cries. It turns a deep red, and still does to this day, except it is a little more faint now. We learned quite a bit and were thankful for her patience in answering our questions.

The doctor needed to jot down notes so she needed Everly to lie down but Everly had other ideas. She lurched away and screamed as if she was on fire. I jumped and reached for her, tears suddenly springing to my eyes, and Vince sat frozen in shock at the lungs on our girl.

All the doctor did was chuckle and calmly say, "Lucky parents. This girl has a set of lungs on her."

She finished her evaluation and we dressed Everly back in her cute flowery dress, which was easier said than done as she squirmed and fussed. After thanking the doctor profusely for answering all our questions and assuring us everything was normal, we walked out into the waiting room to meet back up with my mom.

When we rounded the corner, my mom looked up and laughed. "Was that Everly I heard screaming?"

"Yep," I said.

"How did you know?" Vince asked her.

Mom shrugged. "I recognized it. It's shocking to me how I can already distinguish her cries from other babies."

It was day two, but we felt as if we had always known her.

Our agency guide left while we waited for the paperwork to be finalized. We were to meet up with him a couple hours later at the US Embassy. After being handed a large envelope filled with paperwork and medical records, we headed out to get lunch and relax at the hotel until the Embassy meeting. By the time we made it back to the hotel, Everly was traumatizing the people in the lobby and her new parents with screams of hunger. We had fed her in the waiting room just two hours prior, and she was currently eating every three to four hours, but she was ready and wailing. I mean WAILING.

Japanese formula comes in little blocks of powdered formula that has to dissolve in extremely hot water, then cool down so the baby can drink it comfortably. Yeah, I know what you're thinking...that sounds like quite the process. It was. It could take fifteen to twenty minutes to prepare a bottle. And unfortunately, we were not quick enough that day.

We rushed into the lobby. Those waiting quietly stepped aside to allow us to take the first available elevator. We quickly thanked them as we dashed inside while Everly continued to screech. We had a thermos of hot water, but it had cooled too much and was not fully dissolving the formula in her bottle. Once in the room, Vince poured bottled distilled water into a teapot and set it on the hot plate the hotel provided. It took approximately two minutes to warm the water enough, but it felt like a lifetime. I had no idea a baby could produce a scream as loud as what we were currently hearing from Everly. Once the water was hot, we poured it into her bottle that my mom had just cleaned out and waited for it to dissolve. We all three watched it without blinking until the process was complete, then we shook it vigorously and placed it in the refrigerator to cool it faster. A few minutes passed with me bouncing Everly to soothe her. Finally, the bottle had cooled just enough. Everly sucked the bottle dry and smiled, as happy as could be.

Vince even commented, "Food motivates me too, baby girl."

By the time we were exiting the hotel for the Embassy later that day, which was only two blocks from our hotel, it was raining. We happened to have timed our visit perfectly with the monsoon season which is the most humid time of the year in Japan. So when it was not unbearably hot and suffocating, then it was storming and raining so hard I contemplated building an ark.

I feel I should explain that my mom and I are just not people who can throw on a hat and still look cute in the pouring rain. We actually hate those people. Okay, we don't actually hate them...just a little jealous of anyone who doesn't look like a drowned rat after standing for less than five minutes in the rain.

We decided to hop in a taxi for the quick two block jaunt in order to avoid getting drenched. Once our taxi came to a halt in front of the US Embassy, we realized we had to wait in line outside the building...in the downpour. Luckily, my mom had packed a small umbrella, and we had a larger one from the hotel. So there we were, the three of us and our baby girl, standing under two umbrellas while the wind practically ripped them from our grasp.

Our guide found us in line and stood with us under his umbrella. Being a native of Tokyo, he was unfazed by the rain pelting him in the face every time he turned to carry on a conversation with us, an unwavering smile on his face the entire time. Finally, we reached the building. They informed us we were not allowed to bring in the umbrellas, but had to leave them in a container outside the building.

At this point, I'm sure you are wondering why I keep mentioning the umbrellas. I understand they were only umbrellas. But my mom can come off a little controlling when she is nervous, and she was jet lagged and uncomfortable in a foreign country, along with being stressed out from the entire process in general. She may or may not have thrown what some might consider an adult version of a toddler tantrum.

Our guide from the agency seemed a little confused by her reaction. Eventually, they explained we could get them back upon exiting the building after our interview. If only they would have told us that at the beginning. Instead, they had said, "Must leave umbrella for good in container." You can see why my mom was afraid she wasn't getting it back for the return trip to the hotel.

My exhausted mom threw her hands in the air as she proceeded to walk into the waiting room and have a seat next to a large window. She then muttered to herself, "If they are even still there when we go to leave. That's the only umbrella we packed."

My anxiety hit me hard. I was panicking that the Embassy would have my mom escorted out. People in Japan are very respectful and very soft spoken, unlike some of us Americans, and I was concerned they would see her as being disrespectful. I knew she was just anxious about this whole process. I walked over and sat next to my mom.

"I should have stayed at the hotel and taken a nap," Mom replied. "I'm tired, I'm frustrated, I'm hot as hell in this humidity, and now I look like a wet dog." While it may not sound like it here, Mom definitely meant this as an apology and her tone was one of sincerity. I can't blame her — I'm exactly like her in stressful situations. We really don't mean to come off rude, but our anxiety sometimes brings out the worst in us.

This response was so like her that I tried not to laugh — I really did. But my exhaustion and anxiety bubbled over and escaped in the form of laughter. She rolled her eyes at me and then laughed too.

Of course, I thought the Embassy workers might think we were all crazy and kick us all out, telling us there was no way they would approve us to adopt this little girl who was staring up at me with a look of uncertainty. She was getting really good at giving us that look. And that made me laugh even harder.

118

I think our poor guide was scarred for life by us, but looking back, we were sleep-deprived, anxious, and worried something would go wrong. Human nature was at work again. The only way I knew to cope with my overflow of emotions was to laugh at the absurdity of our situation. Mom's way of dealing with it was to try to control everything she could, and when they said she could not keep that umbrella, she felt out of control.

Eventually, we settled down and were playing with Everly and talking to our guide about life in Japan versus life in America. We discussed the adoption process and the agency and the influx of little ones recently born awaiting families domestically and internationally. I was excited for all the families I had made friends with behind us on the list, while simultaneously praying for those brave first mommas whose hearts were broken.

After approximately thirty minutes, we heard our names called in broken English, and Vince, Everly, and I made our way up to the window where the sweetest, kindest Japanese man smiled at us.

He commented, "Oh, she has the curly hair! And wow, those cheeks!"

We were getting used to those comments. We smiled and told him how we loved both.

He grinned and said, "Yeah, me too."

He then asked us if we intended to give Everly a loving home and provide for her needs. We said yes of course and signed our names.

Then a friendly American took his place. He asked us several more questions about our intentions and the history of Everly's first mom. The agency guide helped answer some of those questions and we held our right hands up and promised to love and provide for our daughter. We signed a few more papers, handed him the packet of information we had been given earlier at the medical office, and thanked the man profusely when he told us that was all he needed. He was going to get her Visa made and would be with us within an hour.

There was a weight lifted from my shoulders immediately after hearing those words. I felt so much lighter knowing the interview we had been dreading was over. It was so much easier than I had expected; they had approved us and were getting all our immigration paperwork ready for our flight home. I could breathe. Finally.

Everly fell asleep on my chest as we waited. The kind Japanese man with the brilliant smile called us up again, handed us an envelope we were not allowed to open until arrival at immigration once we landed on American soil, and told us congratulations. We were officially one step closer to heading home.

We thanked our guide sincerely and made our way to the exit. Once at the exit, we grabbed our umbrellas. Mom was floored that they had not been stolen, but I reminded her that life in Japan is much different than life in America. Thankfully, the rain had stopped, so we walked back to our hotel and enjoyed the sights. The day seemed much brighter.

Japanese Imperial Gardens

Later that night, we ventured to Tokyo Tower and fell in love with the view of Tokyo from so high up. We were happy and relaxed and finally enjoying our time in Japan.

Unfortunately, that night Everly did not sleep as well as she had the night before. She howled and tossed and fought me hard as I held her tightly. At the time, I thought something was wrong, but looking back now, I have a feeling her little heart and soul was processing her trauma and loss. Even as a three-month-old, trauma and loss can affect the brain, and this sweet girl had been through so much in her short three months of life. She had lost her first momma, then was thrown into the loving, but unfamiliar arms of nannies for several days at the agency, and then was placed in our arms. To her, we were just another set of arms to hold her for the time being...she had no idea that we were going to stay. She was processing it all and my heart breaks thinking about it even today as I type these words.

Not only was she dealing with trauma, but she was also extremely stuffy and seemed congested. On day one in our care, we also noticed she already had her two front bottom teeth and seemed to be in pain from possibly more teeth pushing their way through. Vince decided to go out and search for a drug store in the middle of Tokyo at ten at night for infant Tylenol or something similar. I decided to try to clear up her congestion by going into the bathroom and turning on the shower as hot as I could to build up steam.

After bouncing her in my arms with tears streaming down my face and hers in the hot, steam-filled bathroom for twenty minutes, she fell asleep in my arms. I noticed she was clinging to the necklace I had recently begun wearing around my neck. It was a photo of Stormy that my sister-in-law, Erica had given me as a way to always have him with me. My tears flowed even harder at this. Everly and I had both gone through seasons of great loss and now...a newfound connection with each other. We were both beautifully broken.

Vince returned a little after eleven with nothing in hand. Apparently, after using his Google translate app, he discovered that infant Tylenol is not a thing in Japan. It is not legal to give any type of over-the-counter medication to infants. So we sucked it up and took turns bouncing our girl all night long in the bathroom with the steam. It was exhausting and frustrating because we could not make her feel better, but it was also crucial to our bonding with her. I hoped in some small way this was showing her we were here for her and were not leaving.

CHAPTER 12

BLESSINGS AND BLOWOUTS

Morning came and day three began. In hindsight, we should have known things would only get harder as we all adjusted to being a family, but we were so blinded by our relief of having her in our arms, that we decided we would venture out again and do more sightseeing after our meeting at the Japanese agency.

The first stop was the agency office building where we needed to get fingerprinted and to sign even more paperwork. Easy enough, right? Nope. Of course it was not easy.

Vince talked us into trying public transportation so we could stop spending so much on taxis. As you can probably guess by now, my anxiety flared up and I was — for lack of a better word — freaking out. I think poor Everly picked up on that as she was strapped in her carrier against my chest. She was getting fussy and fidgety as we climbed quickly aboard the subway-style train.

People stared at the white people with the crying Japanese baby. I became lightheaded and hot and flustered as I felt their eyes on me. I needed off that train and back on solid ground quickly. And looking at Mom, she felt the same as I did. I looked at Vince with panic-filled eyes. We jumped off at the next stop, found a taxi, and gave our driver the address.

We were already running behind at this point, and once there, the driver, who spoke very little English, told us he thought the agency was in the white, large, nondescript building across the street.

He thought?

So Mom, Vince, and I climbed out of the taxi and crossed four lanes of traffic in Tokyo to this building that had no signs or numbers or information at all. My breath hitched and I began to feel a panic attack brewing. We tried asking people where the agency was located, but nobody seemed to know. They tried helping us and were so kind, but had no idea where the actual office was.

At this point, the social worker who brought Everly to us at the hotel, messaged me on social media asking where we were. The Japanese people are very punctual and we were now almost thirty minutes late.

I explained our situation and she told us to walk up the stairs to our left and take the elevator up one more story and turn right. The entire way, not one sign was seen. Even the main door to the office had no sign. I had no idea how anyone found the place.

Once inside, I felt myself physically relax as I looked at pictures lining the walls of families created because of our two agencies working together. I saw artwork from kiddos who had been adopted and were now older. I saw so many friendly faces doing all they could to take care of babies and find homes for the little ones in their care. I knew our girl had been taken care of those days she was with them.

We signed forms, took pictures, and put our fingerprints on more paperwork. They told us and Everly goodbye and there were plenty of tears shed from everyone. We could tell they loved our girl.

That was it. Now, the only thing left was to go through immigration upon landing on American soil.

We chose to enjoy the rest of the day and Thursday sightseeing before our plane left early Friday morning. Our next stop after returning to the hotel to feed Everly was to head to the local Babies R Us.

So Babies R Us...that was a fun experience...said no one ever. We had to go into a mall to find the Babies R Us, and wow was that a madhouse.

The mall? Talk about sensory overload. The few days we had been in Tokyo, we noticed that there were very few children around and even fewer toddlers and infants. Japan has certain areas that are more kid-friendly than others. The mall was definitely a kid-friendly zone. Toddlers, infants, and teens, were everywhere, running, screaming, dancing, playing.

I just stood there staring once we walked through the doors. I am not exaggerating when I say it was similar to walking into a pit of wild animals compared to the rest of Tokyo we had experienced thus far. We made our way through the throng of people, teenagers, and children to our destination. And I kid you not, Babies R Us was even worse.

I looked at Mom and said, "Okay, let's go. I can't even think in here."

Mom and Vince laughed at me like I was joking. I was not joking.

But I followed them into the bright, overly-colored, loud abyss known as Babies R Us. This Babies R Us was like nothing I had ever seen. It was similar to walking into a techno club, except there were tiny little humans and an endless supply of baby items in every color imaginable. It took us almost an hour to find larger pajamas, teething toys, and a bottle she was more used to versus the bottles we brought that she did not seem to care for.

Somehow, Everly slept in the carrier strapped to my chest the entire time as I clung to the wall hoping to blend in and not be run over by moms and their children.

Thank goodness for my mom. She took control and found every item we needed and actually seemed unfazed by the chaos ensuing around us. I think her nerves, as well as mine, had settled some after finalizing the paperwork.

Shibuya Crossing

"Okay," Mom said, "I think we are good to go."

After eating a wonderful dinner in a small restaurant in the mall, we went back to the hotel to drop off our bags and change clothes. We seriously had to change our clothes once or twice a day because of how badly we were sweating in the unbearable humidity. Then we got the brilliant idea to venture out to Shibuya Crossing.

For those unaware of what Shibuya Crossing is like, it is Japan's version of Times Square. Picture skyscrapers, bright lights, horns blaring, people and cars everywhere — it is just completely overwhelming. But it is so amazing and breathtaking to see in person and should, in my opinion, be on everyone's bucket list.

We decided to cross the street with the horde of people. It was as if we were salmon swimming upstream, but at the same time, it was oddly organized. We made it across while snapping selfies on our cellphones and recording it like all tourists do, right? We went into one of the world's largest Starbucks and watched and recorded people crossing in all different directions. It was incredible to see from above. Then we purchased a couple Starbucks Tokyo mugs, and some warm beverages of some sort, and decided to check out the bookstore that was connected while drinking said beverages.

Everly was strapped to Vince this time since she was on me all morning and afternoon. After about fifteen minutes of browsing, Vince said,

"Ashley, I think Everly may need a diaper change."

I thought, okay, easy enough.

Nope. Once again, it was not easy at all.

In America, you walk into the bathroom and use a changing table to change your baby's diaper. In Japan, very few places have changing tables. We could not find a place to change her. Mom said, "Well, let's go back to the very back and just lay her on my jacket and change her on the floor."

I was very unsure of this idea. All I could picture was a very friendly Japanese security guard escorting us out. But by this point, Vince was literally gagging at the smell and Everly had begun to cry from feeling uncomfortable. So I shrugged and hesitantly agreed.

Once in the back, behind the last row of books, we began to unstrap her from Vince. At that point, I felt bad for laughing, because now I was also gagging and about to vomit because of how strong the smell was.

My mom rolled her eyes and chuckled at the pair of us and went to grab her from Vince. That's when we noticed this was not just a normal dirty diaper. This was what we call "a blowout." It was all over her clothes and the carrier, and unfortunately, also all over Vince.

Now Mom was gagging as well. Yep. Three adults gagging over this cute little chunky baby's dirty diaper in the middle of a bookstore in one of the busiest areas of Tokyo. I can laugh now, but at the time, I was disgusted, worn out, utterly embarrassed, and felt helpless.

The only thing we could do was strap her back into the carrier and hop in a taxi to get back to the hotel pronto. So against Vince's protests, that's exactly what we did. That poor taxi driver probably thought we were lunatics. Vince and I sat in the back with Everly. She was uncomfortable and crying and squirming the entire fifteen-minute ride back. And every time she squirmed, Vince and I gagged while Mom chuckled from the front seat. I am fairly confident the driver drove well above the speed limit (and may have even run a couple stop signs) in order to get us back to the hotel in record time.

We thanked him profusely after he screeched to a stop at the hotel lobby doors, and we ran to the elevator. At this point, the hotel staff at the front desk was used to us Americans and just smiled, waved, and said hello as we ran past throwing out a hello in return.

We closed the door to our room and began unstrapping her from Vince in the bathroom. We stripped her down and gave her a bath in the sink. She laughed as Mom and I plugged our noses while bathing her. It was the first time we heard her laugh out loud and it was a beautiful sound. We got her all cleaned up and then Vince hopped in the shower afterward. We proceeded to throw all the clothes away and get into bed for the night.

Everly had a peaceful night, most likely because she finally had a massive bowel movement, and so did we. Well, we slept well too...we did not have massive bowel movements. I think you get what I mean here. I fell asleep giggling to myself at our eventful night. So far, we had been parents for three days and had experienced teething, crying all night, a hungry baby, a stuffy baby, and a massive blowout.

All of these events are normal and expected, I am well aware, but it is so much more difficult to navigate those events in a foreign country, in a hotel room, thousands of miles from home and comfort. It's a whole added level of stress on top of becoming new parents to begin with. But we survived and these are the memories we can now laugh and tell our Everly about one day.

Becoming a new parent is hard no matter if you are delivering a child or adopting a child. But as new parents, we live, we learn, and we get to share our wisdom with other new parents. No matter how difficult or impossible it seems at times, it is also the most rewarding thing I have ever done. My daughter is my biggest blessing, even during the difficult times and the massive blowouts.

CHAPTER 13

THE JOURNEY ENDS

One Big Happy Family Finally[11]

"So exactly two weeks ago from this very moment (11:00 am Tokyo time on Monday, August 14), we were holding our baby girl for the very first time. A few have asked us what that moment felt like...I honestly cannot describe it. I'm sure for me it was much different than what most experience. My anxiety had me a ball of nerves. I was happy, terrified, sad, nervous, anxious, elated, worried, and the list goes on. I wish I could have focused solely on the good feelings, but those other feelings all crept inside and took hold of me throughout our week in Tokyo.

Yes, we had an amazing time experiencing our little girl's birth country and bonding with her, but to be completely transparent, becoming a first-time parent in a hotel room in a foreign country is so incredibly difficult. I have no words to even describe how hard it really is. There was no way to have some alone time when feeling overwhelmed. We all got on each other's nerves while at the same time realizing the magnitude of this moment. Looking back on it now, it feels as if that week never really happened....it seems like a dream or something I read about in a book. We have

---

[11] *Our blog post on our website posted on August 27, 2017.*

been waiting for this moment for so long, and we tried to soak it all in, but those days were so long, yet flew by in the blink of an eye.

Oh, and to go along with the "becoming first-time parents being hard thing," becoming a parent anywhere is hard, so I have also learned not to judge anyone. There were things I swore I would never do as a parent that I have already done. Desperate times demand desperate measures. So my advice is to prepare as much as you can, then throw out all expectations, because your little one will determine exactly how you will parent."

Thursday, August 17, was our last full day in Japan. We spent it sightseeing, buying souvenirs, and just breathing without the fear that something would go wrong. It felt so freeing knowing we were finished with the paperwork. For the first time in a long time, I felt light and began to relax.

We visited the Skytree, a huge structure where you can see 360 degree views of Tokyo. I have no words to describe the breathtaking views from every angle of the observatory. You realize how truly small you are when looking down on a city the size of Tokyo. I could have spent hours there just taking it all in. Everly was not nearly as impressed and slept comfortably on Vince's shoulder for the entire hour and a half we spent gazing out over the city.

We also took a trip to the Imperial Palace and explored the gardens. The koi ponds and bonsai trees were amazing and so incredibly peaceful. It helped that there was no rain for once and the humidity, though still high, was a little less intense than it had been the previous days. We could actually enjoy the beautiful scenery, and the photos we took that day are

The Imperial Palace

some of my favorites.

After leaving the serenity of the Imperial Gardens, we hopped into a taxi, because after the day before, I refused to use public transportation again. But the ride back to the hotel included a near-death experience... Our taxi driver was just the sweetest and kept looking back at our sweet Everly while she cooed against my chest in her carrier. He was perfecting his English and was carrying on a lovely conversation with us until he went to turn and did not see a guy crossing the road on a bicycle. I saw him though and proceeded to scream, "Watch out!" possibly a little too loudly.

He slammed on the brakes and I hit the back of the driver's seat. The poor guy on the bike wasn't even fazed though he had a near-death experience, but it certainly had my heart racing. Everly cried because my scream had startled her, and the poor taxi driver apologized over and over.

"Oh, no. I am so sorry! So sorry!" he chanted.

"It's okay, really," I replied more than once trying to assuage his concerns. And it was okay...nobody was hurt and it added to a list of stories to bring home from our time in Tokyo, but my heart was racing from adrenaline.

Everly and Vince enjoyed a short nap while my mom and I decompressed some by scrolling through social media. Then we decided to head to Sensoji Temple to pray for a safe journey home and purchase souvenirs from one of the countless shops that lined the path to the actual entrance of the temple.

Sensoji Temple was awe-inspiring. The shops were bustling and a bit overwhelming, but I never felt anxious or unsafe. It was so pleasant watching so many people going all different directions shopping and mingling, while being kind and polite to one another. We bought Everly and myself beautiful kimonos, in which we took photos to celebrate her second year home in August of 2019, and a few other gifts for loved ones. The temple itself was beautifully intricate and we truly felt complete peace as we prayed. Prior to leaving for Japan, we were told by other adoptive families in our program, that it is a sort of tradition to stop there before leaving Tokyo to pray for a safe journey home and for good fortune.

Sensoji Temple

We were informed at the entrance that the Sensoji Temple is one of the oldest (over 1,400 years old) and most famous temples in Tokyo. It is a Buddhist temple dedicated to the goddess of mercy, and the Japanese people travel there to pray for good fortune. Protocol is to cleanse yourself by washing your hands in the water with the dipper provided and then to toss a few coins into the offering box before praying for whatever good fortune you wish to have. We had a wonderful day, and one last delightful, uneventful night at Tokyo Tower where we ate dinner and enjoyed the view of the Tokyo skyline from the top.

That last night in Tokyo, Everly slept well. Vince slept well. Gigi (the name my mom decided to go by for grandma) slept somewhat well. But I slept very little.

My mind was replaying the last year over and over like a film stuck on repeat. The good, the bad, the ugly. It was all there. I allowed the tears to fall, silently grieving all we had lost and celebrating all we had gained. I was excited to be going home, but sad to be leaving my daughter's first home. I couldn't wait to get her home and introduce her to the rest of her family, but was consumed with almost paralyzing sorrow for her first momma, who I had grown to love so much without ever even meeting her. The emotions were fighting each other over which one would consume me the most.

As the waves of grief for our daughter and her first mom crashed over me, the love for our "beautiful moon" kept me afloat. Her name was so perfect, because she seemed to light up the darkness that had been consuming our lives for the last several months. The tears continued to fall that night as I lay there, but not all of them were from sadness...some were from the sheer joy and relief that we were taking our daughter home.

> "Many people have asked us if we had the opportunity to meet Everly's birth mom. We did not. We wanted to meet her so badly, but it just did not work out for many reasons, some of which are not our story to share. She did leave us some of our baby girl's first belongings. We have them put up in a secure box and will give them to Everly when she is a little older. She will always know how much her mother loved her and how brave and selfless her mother must have been."

On top of those emotions, I was terrified of flying home the next morning. As I have mentioned, flying is almost debilitating to me as it is, but now we would be flying with an infant for twelve hours straight. I was so afraid of her throwing a tantrum and causing a scene of gargantuan proportions. There was no other way home, yes, I knew this, but that did not stop me from dreading it.

So when my alarm buzzed loudly at 6:00 am, I had yet to fall asleep. I was beyond exhausted physically, but also mentally and emotionally. I was searching deep within myself for the strength to pull myself from the bed. But as we all do, even in times of great upheaval, I did.

While my beautiful daughter slept blissfully in her bassinet, the three of us got up, got ready, packed up everything, and ordered room service of french toast and fruit one last time.

At nine that morning, we said goodbye to the room where we became parents, to our hotel, and to the amazing staff who took such exceptional care of us. The two front desk attendants said in unison as if they planned it, "Goodbye! We will miss you!"

I refused to allow myself to look back as we drove off in the back of the bus destined for the airport an hour away. I vowed to only look forward from that moment on. There was no point in dwelling in the past. For someone like me, someone who suffers from anxiety, it is better to focus on what I can control and look to the future. The past cannot be changed, and while I still look back fondly sometimes and shed tears, I try to focus more on the good things yet to come. We had a beautiful daughter to raise and so many good memories yet to make with her. That was the reason I smiled as I exited the bus and walked into the airport headed for home.

I could tell you the plane ride was uneventful, that Everly slept the entire time, that we caught up on some rest ourselves, and everyone around us loved us. But that would be a lie.

We sat down and could not find enough room for our luggage in the overhead compartments. The flight attendant raised her voice at us about it, and of course, I cried. That's just my default reaction. As you have probably gathered by now, I cry if I'm happy, sad, scared, embarrassed, nervous...you get the picture.

We finally took our seats and fed Everly a bottle during take-off so her ears would not hurt as badly. She sat and slept for the first hour and a half in the bassinet the airline provided us. It was the only bit of peace we had. An hour and a half in, she began to cry...and cry hard.

The father across the aisle looked at us with a pitying expression while holding his own infant son. "It is what it is," he said. "Eventually she will stop or we will land."

He was right about that I guess. At the moment, I remember thinking that I wished I saw things in black and white like that instead of constantly overthinking everything. Eventually everything ends, so we just needed to hold it together until the plane landed.

For the remaining ten hours, Vince had to stand with her off and on to keep her calm and asleep. She wanted nothing to do with me, which hurt my ego slightly as well. We fed her three bottles, played with her for a while when she was awake and would let Vince sit with her, and cleaned another diaper that almost rivaled the Starbucks incident.

People near us were annoyed. Some pitied us. I was so embarrassed. It was not fun. It was not easy. It was downright awful at times. But we survived. No matter how unpleasant a situation is, we can overcome it. We may not always enjoy the journey, but we will survive it, and maybe even come out stronger because of it.

We landed in Houston, Texas before noon central time, beyond tired at this point. In Tokyo, it was midnight and we would have been in bed. I had been awake for almost thirty-six hours at that point and was nearly stumbling over my own feet walking through the airport.

For those who do not know, when you land on American soil from an overseas flight, you have to go through customs and then back through security again. Yeah, we'd forgotten about that. We stood in line for customs for over an hour with our unopened packet from the Embassy in Tokyo and our sleeping baby girl. Yeah, now she was Sleeping Beauty...on the plane she had been more like Maleficent.

Customs was bad. The man behind the glass divider looked at the paperwork and at Everly's Visa silently with a scowl on his face for several minutes. Vince tried to make small talk, but the man just glared at him and refused to respond. He seemed to love his job (insert sarcasm). I was shaky as he continued to look at her picture on the Visa and her in my arms. She had just awoken and was a little fussy.

Everly's Visa photo

Finally, he said, "The problem I am having is that she looks different from this photo. I am just making sure you have the right baby."

My eyes widened and I gasped slightly. I tried explaining. "Well, in the photo you have, she is laying on a bed and her hair is laid out on top of her head, so it seems like a lot more hair than she really has. We have her hair fixed and back with a little bow right now. Maybe that's it?" I recognized that I was rambling.

He nodded slightly, looked over at her and then down at the green card in his hand one last time, and then entered something into the computer. I was afraid he might be alerting security. But he handed us back our paperwork and Everly's green card and smiled for the first time.

"Okay," he said, "You may go. Congrats!"

I sighed from relief, as did my mom and Vince, and we grabbed our bags and headed up the escalator to baggage claim.

Once we picked up our checked luggage at baggage claim, we headed to security. This was the point where all three of us had breakdowns. I know what you are most likely thinking, "Why couldn't three adults just suck it up and get it together?" But the exhaustion, stress, and emotions were just too much.

When going through security, the agents saw something in one of our bags. They took us to the side and questioned us about what it could be. We truly did not know.

One woman asked us harshly, "I am going to ask you one more time before we search your bags, do you have a water bottle or anything similar in that bag?"

"No, ma'am," I stuttered.

She sighed dramatically and told the man holding our bag to start searching.

They searched and searched and finally found a half empty water bottle the flight attendant gave us on the plane ride from Japan to Texas that we used for Everly's bottle.

It was an accident, but the TSA worker seemed to me unnecessarily condescending when she said, "Hmmm, look what we found."

Before anyone jumps to conclusions, I do respect the work TSA does, and I also understand that security is their job. We had to hold it together and bite our tongues because we were scared of being detained. As mentioned previously, Mom and I do not handle these situations well, and Vince was beyond frustrated and exhausted from the long flight by this point.

As we collected our bags from security, Mom had a minor meltdown because she dropped a bag as we were rushing to catch our connecting flight and everything started to fall out, Vince raised his voice in frustration at us for being so panicked, and I just cried over the idea that we might miss our flight. It was awful. I still cringe when reliving those moments.

In the chaos, Vince left one of our bags outside security, and we were now running behind for our connecting flight. He went clear back to security on the other side of this massive airport to retrieve it.

Mom and I waited for him until last call. Before rushing off to collect our missing bag, he told us to go ahead and he would catch the first available flight, but I refused to leave him. Thank God, we had a stroke of luck. Instead of making him go back through security with the bag, the head of security had cleared it already after finding it unattended, assuming it was a bomb threat, so once Vince got to where we had left it, security released it and drove him frantically back to our gate. He made it with just two minutes to spare before they closed the doors. We walked on the plane and people cheered that we made it on time. They soon would regret that cheer...

This was one of those tiny planes with little to no extra room. I was shaking and felt sick from the turmoil of the last hour and was quite literally holding back vomit. Everly picked up on my emotions. Vince was flustered and angry and practically in tears himself. Mom was frustrated, annoyed, and also crying. Apparently, all three of us are not good in crisis situations.

Everly screamed louder than I have ever heard a baby scream for the duration of the two-hour flight. Vince walked and bounced her up and down the narrow aisle as I sat and hid my face from the people near me. They were asking for headphones to block out her crying. I felt awful and so guilty for causing her so much anguish.

This was the moment I questioned what the heck we had done. What were we thinking? We could not handle this. She would have been better off with another family who had no "issues." Those thoughts raced through my mind during the last flight. But looking back now, I realize that was the anxiety and fatigue talking. I'm sure most parents have questioned their ability to raise good little humans at least once, and if we are being honest with ourselves, probably at least once a week. All parents want the best for their children. I know now these thoughts didn't make me a bad parent, they made me real and, dare I say it, a good parent for wanting Everly to have a stable family who could give her everything she deserved.

After what felt like the longest two hours in history, we landed in Ohio. Vince's mom, his sister Haley, and her boyfriend were waiting for us, along with my brother. We plastered smiles on our faces and laughed at all the right times. I look back at photos of our homecoming now and can see it in our eyes. We have smiles on our faces, but our eyes show our uncertainty. They reveal our anxiety and fear and complete and utter exhaustion. Exhaustion like I have never felt before.

"Oh, my gosh!" Haley exclaimed when she saw Everly in person for the first time.

Vince's mom began to cry when she held her very first granddaughter. "She is just beautiful!"

It felt nice being home around family introducing our girl to them. We were beaming with pride.

The first night home was a whirlwind of meeting aunts and uncles and grandparents. I had never seen my father so excited. The moment he met his first (and still only) grandchild, was unforgettable. All it took was one small smile and giggle when he tickled her and he was head over heels in love. And to this day, she has him wrapped around her tiniest of fingers. Actually, she seems to have that effect on everyone who meets her.

We spent the next week or two getting her adjusted to our schedule and switching her nights and days. It was less difficult than we expected it to be, which was a blessing. Since Vince and I were both trying to coach, neither one of us could take full leave from work. I found myself taking two full weeks off after returning home and then began my partial leave. I stayed home with Everly Mondays through Wednesdays for eight weeks and worked Thursdays and Fridays so I could have cheer practice on Thursdays and attend football games on Fridays.

I felt cheated at the time, because I had to leave her two days a week, but looking back, I am actually thankful it worked out that way. It allowed my mom time to ease into caring for her. Thankfully, she was going to be our full-time babysitter, and she began watching Everly every Thursday and Friday. It also allowed me a chance to prepare myself for leaving her every day.

I missed her terribly, but it would have been so much harder to be home with her for a solid two months straight and then abruptly leave every day once maternity leave ended. I now understand the term "mom guilt." I felt guilty while at work because I wanted to be home with Everly, and I felt guilty when I was at home with her, but needed to be grading essays my students had turned in.

We also began to realize the impact our story and our girl had begun to have on our small rural town. She seemed to have her very own fan club. From day one of arriving home, we had to disappoint people who wanted to meet her right away. We kept her cocooned in our little bubble for the first two weeks and then began to let people in slowly.

"Being home has been an adjustment. We are settling into our whole new normal. Vince and I are taking leave a few days a week alternating so that Everly has one of us home with her every day. She attended her first football game and loved her mommy's cheerleaders, and has met all her fur siblings. She thinks they are so funny, and they seem to like her as well. Jackie isn't too concerned, just a little curious. Sadie can't get enough of her and has become her little protector. The kitties are curious, but keep their distance. Everly seems to be amazed by TVs and cell phones. She loves laughing and smiling, "talking," and playing with her little hands. She also enjoys eating and sleeping...thank goodness!"

Everly loved meeting everyone and enjoyed accompanying us to restaurants, shopping, and even to Friday night football games. She impressed everyone who met her. And I must say I was quite shocked by how quickly I went from being "Ashley" or "Mrs. Banion" to "Everly's mom."

Vince and I were even stopped at our local Walmart one night by someone we recognized but didn't know by name. She went on and on about how she followed our journey on our blog and how happy she was for us. I can only imagine what our faces looked like, because we were shocked by the whole incident. My initial reaction was to be frightened, but then I realized that if she could create this type of impact on others at three months of age, our daughter was going to move mountains one day. And now that she is older and I see more and more of her personality showing itself, I believe this even more strongly. She is made to accomplish great and impossible things. I am so happy and thankful we have a front row seat to everything she will become.

"These days have been amazing, but also so hard for me. There have been so many people pass away over the last few months that I wish would have gotten the chance to meet Everly. She would have charmed them all just like she has charmed everyone else who has met her. Even though I know this is impossible, she

139

seems to know Stormy, too. When we got home that first night, she stared at the painting of Stormy hanging in my living room. She pointed and cooed. She stares at it all the time. One day she will hear all about Stormy...she will know that he is her little guardian angel. Who knows, maybe she does know him...my heart would like to believe that. She shares a part of his name, so maybe she shares a lot more with him as well."

Was our journey of becoming parents and bringing our daughter home exhausting and even excruciatingly difficult at times? Of course. Was it worth it? Absolutely.

I want you to understand that it's okay to fall to your knees and pray for something harder than you have ever prayed before, just to feel paralyzing fear and uncertainty once those prayers have been answered. It's okay to doubt yourself — that's human nature, but please do not judge yourself for those moments of weakness. Give yourself some grace. It's in those moments of weakness that you become stronger. Those moments define you. Moments that take your breath away and help you realize how beautiful life truly is.

Once again, I am actually thankful for the hard times we experienced. When another mom messaged me while in Japan a few months after we had returned home, she was desperate to feel some camaraderie. She was questioning everything and struggling to bond with her baby. I reassured her that it was the stress of becoming a new parent in hotel room thousands of miles from home. I tried to calm her fears by telling her how wonderful the first couple months home had been after a very trying time in Japan. I let her know she was not alone and that we had similar feelings and doubts. Now, after being home for three years, this mom still reaches out to me to let me know how much she appreciated knowing she was not alone in her feelings and that she cannot imagine her life without her little one.

This is one reason I decided to write our memoir. This is the purpose behind laying it all out for you, including the parts that are hard for us to relive and admit to ourselves. I want to encourage you to go after your dreams, whatever they may be, even when those dreams are scary, and even when you doubt that you deserve those dreams to come to fruition.

I'm a dreamer, but I also live in fear most of the time due to my anxiety. I cannot think of anything scarier than becoming a mom or dad for the first time. I am thankful I had my mom and best friends Erica, Kalyn, and Michael to give me advice and encourage me every single step of the way. I could count on my germ-obsessed gal Erica to be the one to inform me of the latest and greatest organic cream for diaper rash. Michael was the friend who would bring me back to reality with her sense of humor and nonchalant attitude. She always made me feel better about making "mistakes." And Kalyn has always been the religious, calming force in my life.

Without these ladies, and my over-protective, always-there-at-any-hour-of-the-day mom, I would have crashed and burned trying to figure out this whole mom gig. The biggest thing I've learned: It's okay to reach out and ask for help. The moment we all stand together and lift each other up is the moment we become empowered and our sons and daughters learn how to be gracious, selfless, and respectful. I am thankful I not only have my closest friends and family members as part of my support system and army, but also a whole community of adoptive moms and dads as well.

> "This journey has been so incredibly difficult for us...not just the adoption, but the entire year has been rough. People told us that there must be one specific child meant to be ours. We believed that, but we had also started losing hope. Adoption isn't easy, but we know without a doubt everything happened because this little girl was meant to be our daughter.
>
> Thank you all for following us and supporting us. This part of our journey has come to an end, but the next chapter is just beginning."

CHAPTER 14

MOVING FORWARD

Reflecting on 2017[12]

> "I'm sitting here on an unscheduled day off from school due to
> frigid temperatures and have been reflecting on this past year
> while holding my little cherry blossom. Maybe it's the new year or
> maybe it is just finally hitting me, but I have been reliving the past
> two years while writing my memoir. Some days I can't even
> believe this is real life; I can't believe that after everything, she is
> really here in our arms. Then there are other days where I feel as if
> she has always been here and has been a part of our family
> forever. I don't know...maybe that's because she was always
> meant to be our daughter...maybe my heart and soul just always
> knew who she was and that we would find each other."

The last four years have been amazing, exciting, terrifying, and at times,
excruciatingly painful. I could write forever about our life at home with our
girl, and maybe I'll write about surviving the first year home someday, but
this is not the time and place for that part of our story.

I used to think everything happens for a reason, and, to some extent, I still
believe that. But I am more guarded now. I am more jaded. I am more
aware and less naive. Instead of saying everything happens for a reason, I

___

[12] *Our blog post on our website posted on January 5, 2018.*

now believe our story was written exactly as it was always meant to be and has unfolded as it was intended to. But maybe there was never a reason for any of it.

I won't say there was a reason for my grandpa dying of cancer a few months before meeting our girl. I refuse to think it was fate that my aunt's wish of meeting our daughter was never fulfilled. I will not pretend to understand why Stormy became so sick and missed meeting our daughter, making our adoption journey that much more mentally and emotionally exhausting. Why did they happen the way they did? What was the *reason*? I have no answers for those questions.

But I don't think I'm supposed to have any answers to those questions really. It's impossible to make sense of tragic events that tear you down and bring you to your knees. Unfortunately, that's the beauty and ugliness of life. The beauty is actually in not knowing what our future holds, the surprises around every bend in the road can take your breath away. But the ugliness of life is never understanding why horrible things happen to people. We are not meant to make sense of it — we are meant to make the most of it and learn from the good times and the bad times. And God willing, one day, you will look back and take it all in and realize you were on one heck of a ride.

> "While reflecting on our journey, we have come to realize several coincidences, or maybe they weren't coincidences, that caused us to realize that we were always right where we were supposed to be — we were always on the right track at the right time, even when we felt lost, discouraged, and scared that we would never bring home a little one. At any rate, I wanted to write them down so that I would never forget the interventions the universe and God made on our behalf so that we could unite with our daughter at exactly the right moment in time. It is so amazing to look back now and understand God, fate, the universe, they all had it planned out...all we really needed to do was sit back and let it unfold...I guess hindsight really is 20/20.
>
> The first divine intervention we recognized is that we filled out our

paperwork to send in to our placement agency on May 11, 2016, exactly one year from the day our girl was to be born. The next is that, in August of 2016, we had our first and only home study visit and on the other side of the world, our daughter's birth mom found out she was pregnant (according to the social report we received). On May 11, 2017 our daughter was born in Japan, and here in the US, Stormy had a great day. He had been having a rough week, but on this day, he seemed so happy and felt so much better. Unfortunately, as you all know, he passed a few days later on May 15, but I am so thankful we had that final great day together. We received our first referral on May 19, which would have been the day our Mizuki was released from the hospital in Japan, and we lost that referral on the 22nd. I felt so devastated, mostly because I felt our daughter had been born. I just could not figure out how and why I felt this way since obviously our child had not been born yet...little did I know what would transpire.

Fast forward to July 2017...we had been informed on Monday, July 24, that once again, the baby that was born the week before would be staying with her birth mom. While we were elated her mom could keep her little one, it was so hard hearing this news over and over again, so I told Kelsey from our agency that we did not want any more updates until the referral was ready for us. I knew it would be hard to be in the dark for several weeks or months, but I just couldn't keep hearing we might have a baby, just to find out we didn't. On July 25 in Japan (July 24 here in Ohio...the same day we said no more updates), Mizuki's birth mom reached out through email to the Japanese agency about an adoption plan for her. On July 26, here in Ohio, I began writing a letter to our future child.

We received a referral in record time, exactly one week from the time the agency in Japan took custody on August 2. We received a referral August 9 and flew out of Columbus on August 12, exactly 15 months to the day that we mailed out our application packet to our agency stateside bringing our whole journey full circle.

144

Coincidence, divine intervention, fate...I don't really know, but I do know that we have the girl who was always meant to be our daughter. I wish we would have had more faith along the journey. We do have unwavering faith now though, because I have never before been so sure of God's plan than after watching our story unfold right before our eyes. What an amazing thing to witness firsthand."

Vince and I learned to navigate life at home with an infant and now a toddler. We (kind of) figured out how to balance work, family, and hobbies. We still struggle with all of that at times, but we know that in order to be truly happy and balanced and the best versions of ourselves, we can't just be Mom and Dad. We have to also be teachers, coaches, writers, photographers, friends, siblings, spouses, and the list goes on.

While we have begun to figure out the technical parts of life and how to balance it all, we still know there will be times we fall and doubt ourselves. But I think that's just life. It's not about how many times you fall down, but how many times you pick yourself up and try again. I'm sure you have all heard some version of that more than once in your life.

I still struggle with anxiety. I have good days and bad days. But never again will I have a day where I want to give up on a goal or dream I have for myself. If I'm feeling anxious, I go outside and jog harder, faster, and longer on my favorite back country road. If I'm angry at myself for dropping the ball on some task I had planned for myself or my family, I suck it up and I try harder to achieve that task the next time. Life is that way. We all falter at times. We all sit in the bottom of the shower (or your safe place) and cry mercilessly sometimes, whether we want to admit it or not. We just need to figure out what works for us, what inspires us to stand up again, and it helps to know you are not alone. I'm here to tell you, you are not alone.

There will be days in our future when we will have to answer some hard questions from Everly, and we are preparing ourselves for the days ahead. She will want to know why her first family could not raise her. She will want to know why we chose to adopt. She might have hard feelings to

Everly's first mom sent us this dress for her.

process and attempt to work through and understand. I am, in a way, dreading those conversations, but I will not shy away from them either. We will be open and honest with her and hold nothing back. She deserves that. She deserves the world.

I just hope and pray that we raise her to know how strong and beautiful she is. I hope and pray she can feel how unconditionally we love her every single day. And more than anything, I want her to know that her past is a part of her story she could not control, but her future can be anything she wants it to be. Everly is already a force to be reckoned with at just three years old, and I know great things are in store for her. It is our job to give her the confidence to believe that about herself and to live and love fiercely and unapologetically.

In the last four years, I have also learned that you never really get over or even move past the grief. It's always there. Instead, you learn to acknowledge it. You learn to accept it. You learn to move forward with the grief. It has now just become a part of who I am.

I think about and remember Papaw Bud, Aunt Ruth, and my Stormy boy, along with all the others I have lost along the way, nearly every day, sometimes multiple times a day. Sometimes I smile, sometimes I cry. That's okay. It doesn't make me weak. It doesn't make me strong either. It just makes me human. It's just who I am now.

Grief changes a person...it certainly changed me. I am no longer the person I was four years ago, but that's okay also. We are meant to grow and change and learn. It is part of what makes us human. It's what makes this journey of life so beautiful and so heartbreaking. The biggest lesson I have learned though is that sometimes a stormy sky can be beautiful, but even when it's not, remember that once those storm clouds roll out, there is always a beautiful moon waiting.

EPILOGUE

HERE AND NOW

Here I am at the end of a memoir I doubted I would ever complete. The magnitude of that is not lost on me. This experience, along with the grief I've had to learn to live with, has taught me that life is short and precious. Why not go after what you want? Why not go after that dream you've had since you were a little girl? My daughter gave me the courage I needed to go after something I have wanted since I was twelve years old and won my first Young Author's writing competition.

Blowing out the candles

Today, Everly is three years old. She is wild and sassy and a lover of life. She likes things to be done her way, and lets us know if she doesn't approve, just as she has since day one together in Tokyo. She is wildly independent, but loves being around her family. She now has three cousins, all boys, on Vince's side of the family, and thinks they are pretty special.

Watching her grow and change has been the most amazing experience in the world. Every single day, we thank God and the universe for her. I also send up a silent thank you every morning, thanking her first momma for choosing us to be her family. I hope in some way, she can feel the unconditional love we have for her.

My anxiety has been well-controlled now for over two years. I am meditating and breathing deeply when necessary, along with jogging and walking at night for at least thirty minutes. I also practice daily gratitude by writing in a journal at least five things I am grateful for each day. This keeps me grounded and focused on the present instead of the future or past, and also has me constantly looking for the good things in my life. Two years ago, I was also diagnosed with hypothyroidism, which causes anxiety and can increase depression. My doctor believes this is the reason why my anxiety began spiraling out of control, along with all the stress and grief 2016 and 2017 brought our way. But I am happy to say I am in a good place, and working every day to stay that way.

Many have been asking what is next for us in terms of additional children. If I am being honest, our plan was to start the adoption process a second time to bring home a sibling for Everly from Japan when she turned three. Unfortunately, those plans have been ripped from us. The Japan program has closed due to changes in adoption laws in Japan, along with the American government making it more difficult for international adoptions to continue. I could write a whole book on this information alone, but for now, I will just say international adoption has slowed tremendously. While one of the reasons for that is because countries are trying to advocate for more domestic adoption, which is amazing news, the other part is the American government has put in place many roadblocks. Roadblocks that many American families cannot work around. While some of these changes are essential in keeping international adoption ethical, in my opinion, some seem to be unneeded and serve only as a barrier for families wishing to bring home a child from another country.

The thought of Everly living her life in an orphanage haunts me at night. The idea of her never knowing the love of a family and the image of her spunky personality being suppressed from life in an orphanage, no matter how well-run the orphanage is, destroys me. The thoughts alone chase my breath away; I literally struggle to catch my breath thinking about it now. There are so many children who now see this as their future, and it breaks me.

So, for now, Japan is no longer an option for us, and that pill is really hard to swallow. We are grieving hard for the life we had hoped for and planned for ourselves. But more than that, we are grieving for those children who will be affected negatively by these changes, and for our Everly. We hate that she will never have a sibling who shares her culture. Vince and I understand how important it is for all kids, but especially adopted children, to have others near them that mirror their culture and life

Everly wearing the kimono that we bought her in Tokyo.

experiences. And while we are keeping in close contact with many families with adoptive children from Japan, we are completely heartbroken. I have spent many nights crying over the future that will now never be.

We have looked into other Asian international programs, but at this time, none of those feel right for us, nor do we fit the criteria for certain countries. Korea is our best fit, but with the stigma surrounding anxiety there, I may not get approved to adopt because of my past and current issues. I have spoken to several families and agencies about Korea, and I think it would be amazing, but the idea of getting clear to the end and then not being approved in a courtroom in Seoul after bonding with our son or daughter, would shatter me.

We have also looked into domestic adoption, but after discussing it, we would really like Everly to share a similar ethnicity with her future sibling. Parents of Asian ethnicities make up a very small percentage of domestic adoptions, but that is still an option for us. We would love to give a home to another child in need, but there are just so many unknowns and so much consideration that goes into this very personal decision.

Vince and I are now in a strange spot of not really knowing our next move. For now, we have decided to enjoy our little family of three. Maybe that's all we will always be, and if so, we could not feel more blessed that we get to call Everly our daughter. Right now, we are more focused on how to start discussing adoption with her. We have talked about Japan and have mentioned adoption, but she is still too young to fully comprehend what it all even means. Adoption stories are so complex and so personal, so we will make a plan and adjust as necessary. For now, we just love our girl and are creating the most incredible memories together. We are choosing joy and to cherish every moment.

Maybe we will adopt again in the future from another country or domestically. Or maybe we will foster a child or children one day. Or we will spend our lives doting on our beautiful moon. If we learned anything from our journey to bring Everly home, it was to have patience and to have faith that everything will work out the way it is meant to. So for now, that is what we will do...enjoy every single day, and have faith that things will work out exactly as they are destined to.

ACKNOWLEDGEMENTS

First, I would like to start off by thanking Jonathan at Wordrobe Media for working with me and doing such a fantastic job helping me polish my words and making this memoir the best it could be.

To my parents, I am so thankful for the way you always believe in me and I love that you two are some of my biggest cheerleaders. I would also like to thank my mom for basically helping raise my daughter and my dad for being the one I get my dreamer mentality from. All my love always.

I want to thank my brother for the guidance in helping me complete this project in the "right" way instead of trying to finish it all on my own, and Sanaa for helping guide me with cover advice. You know I adore both of you.

To my mother-in-law...you are always so encouraging and are always ready to help me in any way you can. I won the lottery in the mother-in-law department.

To my three best gals, Kalyn, Erica, and Michael, I would not have had the courage to pursue this dream of mine without your constant encouragement and support. Our girls' days are what reenergizes, decompresses, and fuels me. I love you girls to the moon and back.

Tomomi...you are one of a kind, my friend! I am so thankful our adoption journeys brought us and our daughters together. Pen pals for life!

To Sara and Sarah, you both have shown such courage in your adoption journeys and I am in awe of you both. I am thankful we all have found our happily ever afters, even if they didn't end up as expected. I can't wait to get our kiddos together one day.

Josie, I am thankful for connecting and even more grateful that our girls will grow up knowing one another, even if it is virtually most of the time. I am ready for our in-person meet-up.

152

Kelsey, I have no words for what you mean to me and my family. You are the reason we have our girl. You have literally changed hundreds of lives and that is an understatement. I thank God for you every single day, and I cannot wait for you to meet our girl in person one day very soon. Love you, friend!

To all my other dearest friends I've found recently through the adoption community and those I am lucky enough to have had since childhood (you all know who you are), I hope you always know how much your friendship and support inspires me. And I hope you know you all mean the world to me.

To the members of my launch team, I want to thank you so much for your support and help with bringing this book out into the world. It means more to me than you will ever know.

To Vince, my high school sweetheart and husband, I am blessed to have you, even if I don't always show it. Ha! You are always willing to go along for the ride when I have a crazy dream to chase after. You went all in on this one, and I could not be more thankful, and I could not love you more for that. And I need to give you a shout-out for creating this beautiful cover, even after I had you create about a dozen different options. It is beautiful and exactly what I envisioned.

And to Everly, my reason for breathing, I will never be able to express in words the love I feel for you. You are my why. You are my inspiration. You are my world. I pray you always dream big, sweet girl. I am so thankful to be your momma. I love you more than life…

Stormy boy, keep watching over us until we meet again at the rainbow bridge...I'll forever miss you and love you.

ABOUT THE AUTHOR

Ashley is an 8th grade English teacher, who also coaches high school cheerleading. As a child, Ashley had big dreams of becoming a published author one day, and could think of no better way to accomplish that goal, than to write about the journey to her daughter. Along with teaching, coaching, and living that mom life, Ashley also has a small photography business with her mom and runs her own small bow and hair accessory shop. She enjoys hiking, reading, writing, and scrap-booking as well. Ashley is also a self-proclaimed movie and television enthusiast, with *Friends* being her all-time favorite television series. She lives in central Ohio with her high school sweetheart, Vince, and their daughter, Everly, along with the rest of her family, two horses, one pup, and four cats. You can catch up with her on Instagram and Facebook.

Instagram: Instagram.com/1bighappyfameventually

Facebook: One Big Happy Family, Finally

Made in the USA
Monee, IL
01 December 2020

50404657R00092